KU-133-143

musée**fin-de-siècle**museum

museum guide

muséefin-de-sièclemuseum

museum guide

H A Z A N

Royal Museums
of Fine Arts of Belgium

M. & Mme Gillion Crowet

 belspo

 Regie der Gebouwen / Régie des Bâtiments

 be be.brussels

 National Lottery — creating chances together

 KBR be

 Belfius

 CINEMATEK

National Lottery logo — Koning Boudewijnstichting / Fondation Roi Baudouin

 BIBLIOTHECA WITTOCKIANA

  La Monnaie / De Munt

 ULB

 .be

 Petercam

 TEVEAN

 CHAMPAGNE PERRIER JOUËT

 THALYS

 EUROSTAR

 Villo!

 RÉSEAU ART NOUVEAU NETWORK

 VISITBRUSSELS

 Wallonie-Bruxelles Tourisme

 toerisme vlaanderen

 Become a Friend

 La Prem1ère — Soyez curieux

 arte BELGIQUE

 MU SI Q3

 La Libre BELGIQUE

Knack

LE VIF L'EXPRESS

 COBRA.be

 Klara

 metro

AGENDA

This book has been published to mark the inauguration on 6 December 2013 of the Musée Fin-de-Siècle Museum, of the Musées royaux des Beaux-Arts de Belgique

muséefin-de-sièclemuseum

Director general: Michel Draguet   **Academic coordinator:** Inga Rossi-Schrimpf

REALIZATION

The Musée Fin-de-Siècle Museum has seen the light of day thanks to the dedication and professionalism of the entire team of the Musées royaux des Beaux-Arts de Belgique and the Régie des Bâtiments, as well as the Région de Bruxelles-Capitale, the Politique Scientifique Fédérale, and the various partner institutions and collections. Given below are the names of the managers of the different departments that, with their teams, have brought this project to a successful conclusion.

CURATORS

Inga Rossi-Schrimpf, Dominique Marechal, Francisca Vandepitte

EXHIBITION SERVICE

Sophie Van Vliet, Marie Decoodt

ARCHIVES

Véronique Cardon

ACADEMIC COORDINATOR

Jennifer Beauloye

RESTORATION AND CONSERVATION

Coordinator: Brita Velghe
Restorers: Sarah Benrubi, Derek Biront, Christian Copet – Maison Copet le Grelle & Associés SPRL, Chantal Fontaine, Jean-Albert Glatigny, Alain Milhau – Maison André, Julie Swennen, Étienne van Vyve
Collection guards: Frank Horemans, Eddy Hiernaux, Jean-Marie Schoumaker, Ludovic Godfrin, Stéphane Vandemaele, Yvon Lespagne

SECRETARIAL SERVICES

Patricia Robeets, Marleen Madou

BACKUP SERVICES

Colette Janssen

ADMINISTRATION AND FINANCE

Vinciane de Brouwer, Rik Snauwaert, Geert Boets

TECHNICAL STUDIES, SECURITY, COORDINATION AND EXECUTION

For the Musées royaux des Beaux-Arts de Belgique
TECHNICAL SERVICES
Peter Vanhopplinus

TECHNICAL SYSTEMS, COORDINATION AND CONSTRUCTION OF THE EXHIBITION ARCHITECTURE

Operational supervision: Yves Vandeven
Administrative support: Dirk Vleminckx
Studios: Antoine Fasseaux, Luc Denève, Cédric Hubin
Scenography: Thu-Mai Dang
Lighting, electricity, electronics: Rudy Cloetens, Nicolas Mariques, Daniel De Gendt, Serge Hérion
Computer systems: Jack Claeys, Diedrik Van den Driessche
Operational support: Marc Van Hoof, Beny Vermaeren

With the assistance of Pascal Marchant of the Musées Royaux d'Art et d'Histoire

SECURITY

Maarten Lousbergh
Joachim Meert
Ives Breels
Internal security teams

SERVICES TO THE PUBLIC

Isabelle Vanhoonacker

PHOTOGRAPHY DEPARTMENT

Catherine Bourgeois

MULTIMEDIA

Jennifer Beauloye, Jean-Philippe Theyskens, Thu-Mai Dang

SIGN DESIGNERS

Piet Bodyn, Vladimir Tanghe

COMMUNICATIONS, PUBLIC RELATIONS, EVENTS, SPONSORSHIP

Anne Goffart, Caroline Haraké, Camille Préfole, Matyas Fuzfa

PRESS

Barbara Porteman with Séverine Provost, Be Culture

NTERNET SITE

Pierre-Yves Desaive, Karine Lasaracina

EDUCATEAM

Myriam Dom and her team

MUSEUM SHOP

Koenraad Reynaert and his team

WELCOME DESK

Sylviane Van Droogenbroeck, the volunteers of the Amis des Musées royaux des Beaux-Arts de Belgique

BOOKING OFFICE

Laurence Ryckaert and her team

INTERNS

Anca Cercel, Lucie Vallade

INSTITUTIONAL PARTNERS

Belspo
Région de Bruxelles-Capitale
Régie des Bâtiments

Laurent Vrijdaghs, manager, Dirk Van Geystelen, Paul De Ceuster, Jean-Marie Bracke, Marie-Caroline Pardon, Freddy Tavernier, Jochem Naaktgeboren, Chakib Goulmi, Hughes Malherbe, Arbia Nouredinne, Marc Rommens

ORGANIZATIONAL PARTNERS

Bibliothèque Royale de Belgique
Patrick Lefevre, director general
Marie Cornaz, music section
Claude Sorgeloos, rare book section
Joris Van Grieken, prints cabinet
Benoît Labarre, exhibition service

Théâtre Royal de la Monnaie
Peter de Caluwe, artistic director
Jan Van Goethem, archives
Frédéric Delmotte, archives

Musées Royaux d'Art et d'Histoire
Michel Draguet, interim director general
Céline Quairiaux, photographic conservation and restoration

Cinémathèque Royale
Nicola Mazzanti, director
Bruno Mestdagh, collections manager

Belfius Banque
Jos Clijsters, president
Patricia Jaspers, art collection and exhibitions manager

Bibliotheca Wittockiana
Michel Wittock, president
Pauline Loumaye, librarian

Fondation Roi Baudouin
Dominique Allard, director
Julie Lenaerts, collection manager

Université Libre de Bruxelles
Didier Viviers, rector
Alain Delchambre, president of the CA
Patricia Lodzia-Brodski, collections manager

PROMOTIONAL PARTNERS

Visitbrussels, Wallonie – Bruxelles Tourisme, Toerisme Vlaanderen

EXTERNAL PARTNERS

Construction sites: HVAC, AXIMA Contracting
Structural construction: Group Monument, Monument Vandekerckhove
Marble floor: Kreglinger
Light well covering: Veldeman
Electricity: Tevean
Lighting: Huib Nelissen Decor en Constructiewerken
Lighting consultant: Joost De Beij
Painting: Van Meerbeeck
Windows: Meyaert
Lettering: Bulle Color sprl
Transport: Mobull
Insurance: Léon Eeckman Art Insurance
Photographic enlargements: Pelegrie s.a.
Multimedia: Inter2Face
Promotional film: Epic architecture, 3Dynmaqueta, WRKSHP
Film: Yvon Lammens
Audioguides: Espro (editing: Anne Sefrioui)

ACKNOWLEDGEMENTS

Christine Ceulemans, Interim Director General of the Institut Royal du Patrimoine Artistique, Sabine Bompuku Eyenga-Cornelis, Maarten Couttenier, Jean-Philippe Huys, Wilfried Moens, Anne Welschen

PUBLICATION

Editorial coordination: Brigitte de Patoul
Texts: Anne Sefrioui
Copy-editing
Inga Rossi-Schrimpf, Dominique Marechal, Francisca Vandepitte, Jennifer Beauloye, Brigitte de Patoul

ÉDITIONS HAZAN

Editorial coordination: Céline Guichard and Anne-Isabelle Vannier
French-to-English translation: Timothy Stroud
Rewriting: Chrisoula Petridis
Graphic design: Sylvie Milliet
Cover design: Jean-Marc Barrier (poem)
Production: Claire Hostalier and Marie Dubourg

XELLES   Musées Royaux de Peinture et
de Sculpture

FOREWORD

The reorganization of the collections of modern art belonging to the Musées royaux des Beaux-Arts de Belgique has entailed the preparation of a theme-based calendar of which the Musée Fin-de-Siècle Museum is the first stage. In the building constructed by Philippe Robert-Jones and Roger Bastin as a compromise solution to satisfy a public that was then little inclined to accord modern art its full approval, this new museum provides a view of modernity which, at the start of the nineteenth century, had assumed a flowering of new forms to embrace the wave of new ideas and thoughts.

The starting point of the project was the building, whose architectural solutions have been exploited without disrespect to its spirit. The light well has become an amphitheatre which, at the core of the museum, stirs memories of an architecture that has often received poor treatment in Brussels. The rooms have been renovated without giving in to a certain fashion for colourful effects and a revival of kitsch. On the contrary, we have maintained the modern principle that governed the conception of the building inaugurated in 1984. Whereas the walls are not completely white, they are an extension of a certain modernist ideal associated here with the late nineteenth century.

The Musée Fin-de-Siècle Museum does not celebrate 'modern art' but the idea of modernity as it was elaborated in an avant-garde review appropriately called L'Art moderne. With the organization of the Salons des XX (1883-94) and that of La Libre Esthétique (1894-1914) in the very rooms of our museum, Brussels was a crossroads of truly unique creativity. Its artists did not associate themselves with the tidal wave of impressionism alone, but found the emblems of an identity that was largely to determine the appearance of Brussels in the conjunction of symbolism, Wagnerism and art nouveau. 'Brussels, the capital of art nouveau' was not a description related purely to architecture. To start with, the term embraced the dynamism of Brussels society, which was reflected in all domains of creation: literature, painting, opera, music, architecture, photography and poetry. Maeterlinck, Verhaeren, Ensor, Khnopff, Spilliaert, Maus, Horta, van de Velde, Kufferath, Lekeu – the list is not exhaustive but this publication goes into the matter in detail. However, it is indicative of the breadth and depth of Belgian creativity, which overflowed the country's borders to reach deep into Europe, and even around the world, of which the awarding to Maurice Maeterlinck of the Nobel Prize for literature in 1911 is a dazzling example.

This museum rests its validity on the thirty-one salons that drew the essence of European creativity to Brussels. The artists involved revolved around the creation of the Société Libre des Beaux-Arts and the city's art circles which, as from 1868, introduced to Brussels the debate on modernity, the sense of which Charles Baudelaire had only shortly before examined in his Petits poèmes en prose that make up his book Le Spleen de Paris. Modernity, which was growing in vogue, was answered by a dynamic that drew attention within the modern milieu to criticism directed at what was referred to as the 'would-be modern' illusion. Peripheral in comparison to the scene in Paris but central due to its role as a crossroads of Europe, the Belgian art world carried the modern movement forward in all its facets, from avant-garde frenzy to critical backlash.

Providing an account of this artistic phenomenon called for a multidisciplinary approach that could only be provided by a partnership between the Musées royaux des Beaux-Arts, the Bibliothèque Royale, the Théâtre Royal de la Monnaie, the Musées Royaux d'Art et d'Histoire, the Bibliotheca Wittockiana, the Cinémathèque Royale de Belgique as well as the Fondation Roi Baudouin and Belfius Banque, whose collections are demonstrative of the deep roots this fin-de-siècle culture had in Belgium. With our partners we have succeeded in creating an intense and incisive portrayal of this period. With the Gillion Crowet Collection, made possible by the Région de Bruxelles-Capitale, this portrait has turned into a veritable spectacle. The collection is the material face of a collector's passion for a certain historical period, and includes a series of masterpieces that are representative of the unity and creativity of this era. Whereas some would have liked to divide the collection up between the decorative and fine arts, the wish of Anne-Marie Gillion Crowet was to ensure that her selection of glassware, paintings, furniture and silverware remained in a single magnificent presentation illustrative of the aspiration shared by all artists and craftsmen: to produce art that transfigures reality.

I would like to thank my colleagues whose boldness made this daring partnership possible: Mr Patrick Lefèvre, director general of the Bibliothèque Royale; Mr Peter de Caluwe, director of the Théâtre Royal de la Monnaie; Mr Michel Wittock, president of the Bibliotheca Wittockiana; M. Nicola Mazzanti, director of the Cinémathèque Royale de Belgique; Mr Dominique Allard, director of the Fondation Baudouin and Mr Jos Clijsters, chairman of the management committee of Belfius Banque. I am also grateful to Mr Rudi Vervoort, minister-president of the government of the Région de Bruxelles-Capitale, and Mr Guy Vanengel, minister of the government of the Région de Bruxelles-Capitale, in charge of finance, the budget, the civil service and external relations, and administrator of the Gillion Crowet donation in lieu of estate taxes in the new museum. With the gratitude of a friend, I add to their names that of Mr Charles Picqué, who 'imposed' this donation with force and conviction. I am happy to pay tribute here to this lover of art nouveau, who spared no trouble to ensure that the heritage of Brussels was enriched by this collection. I should also like to recognize the work carried out by the members of the committee who oversaw the donation - Pierre Dejemeppe, Anne-Sophie Walazyc, Pieter De Keyser and Guy Conde-Reis of the Région de Bruxelles-Capitale, Frederik Leen of the Musées royaux des Beaux-Arts de Belgique, René Delcourt of the authority responsible for the federation's scientific policy - Mr Gillion Crowet, the family's representative, and the experts Françoise Aubry and Pascale Vandervellen.

Within the context of this donation, I would also like to show my gratitude to the deputy prime minister, Mr Didier Reynders, who, as finance minister, supported the donation project - completed in 2006 - from the first moment.

I am also very obliged to those who followed the project within the institution. Inga Rossi-Schrimpf, who, as project leader, coordinated the whole thing; Francisca Vandepitte and Dominique Marechal, curators; Sophie Van Vliet and Marie Decoodt, from the exhibitions department; Peter Vanhopplinus, head of the technical service and site supervisor; Maarten Lousbergh, head of security; Vinciane De Brouwer, in charge of financial services; Anne Goffart, communications manager; Isabelle Vanhoonacker, who directs the services offered to a growing public; and Colette Janssens, in charge of support services. And through each of these managers I pay tribute to their teams who have worked with such zeal and efficiency. My thoughts also go to my colleagues in our partner institutions who have supported us and contributed to making this dream a reality.

With the staff of the Musées royaux des Beaux-Arts de Belgique I unreservedly associate the Association des Amis who, under the presidency of Mr Philippe Delusinne, support us enthusiastically and effectively. The president is naturally complemented by the board of administration, which positively welcomed the idea to create the Musée Fin-de-Siècle Museum as the first step in the reorganization of our collections of modern art. Particular mention should be made of Christiane Berghmans-Waucquez for the delight with which she developed 'Become a Friend', and Sylviane Van Droogenbroeck, who so proficiently directed the volunteers, the family without which the Musées royaux would not be able to function.

I take the opportunity to thank, in the person of their general administrator, Mr Laurent Vrijdaghs, all the teams in the Régie des Bâtiments for their collaboration.

The staff of the Musées royaux are fortunate to be able to count on their partners to contribute the most advanced equipment to the renovation of the technical plants. I shall end by thanking Éditions Hazan for producing this visitors' guide.

Lastly, it is with feeling that I express my gratitude to our patrons. Roland and Anne-Marie Gillion Crowet, as well as their family, not only built up a unique collection, they have also displayed exceptional generosity in maintaining the magnificence and integrity of this collection, and transferring it from their apartment to the museum, from what Mallarmé called the *grotte d'intimité* to the openness of the public domain.

The end of the century was not synonymous with exhaustion: it was a celebration of the spirit that transcended the harshness of the times. To choose 6 December 2013 to inaugurate a museum that celebrates it is symbolic: a century ago, the Théâtre Royal de la Monnaie was putting the final touches to its production of *Parsifal*, which was to open almost exactly a month later. That day, 2 January 1914, represented the climax of a vast movement initiated more than thirty years earlier. For us who know what followed, the date strikes a tragic chord. Through this museum, one facet of our past is placed in the public spotlight to help reveal to us what we are: it is a brilliant and vibrant past, shot through with light and shadow, dreaming of its future while inventing its origin. An enduring lesson and spectacle at the heart of a European capital now at peace.

Michel Draguet
DIRECTOR GENERAL
MUSÉES ROYAUX DES BEAUX-ARTS DE BELGIQUE

Bruxelles   Square du Mont des Arts.

2 — BRUXELLES - Le Palais de Justice - La Place Poelaert

FIN-DE-SIÈCLE BELGIUM

"Belgium is a magnificent art book whose chapters, happily for the glory of the provinces, are spread all around but whose preface is in Brussels and Brussels alone."

In 1875, it was in these admiring terms that the French painter Eugène Fromentin extolled the splendour of the Belgian capital, the modernization of which Léopold II had been actively leading for ten years: "Belgium is a magnificent art book whose chapters, happily for the glory of the provinces, are spread all around but whose preface is in Brussels and Brussels alone." The "Builder King" wished to make the city where he resided a dazzling showcase for a young and enterprising country where all forces – including those of the cultural domain – were invited to work together to create a national identity.

As the world's second most industrial nation after Great Britain, during this period Belgium enjoyed exceptional prosperity derived from various resources – mining, smelting and textiles in particular – and the animated activity of the port of Antwerp stimulated by the country's first-hand dealings with Africa. Lastly, communications throughout the country were ensured by an extremely dense network of roads, canals and railways. At its centre, Brussels was the city to which both people and investments flocked: it did not cease to grow over the decades, encompassing neighbouring municipalities and rising in number from one hundred and forty thousand inhabitants in 1830 to over half a million by the end of the century.

Demographic requirements and the desire for a prestigious capital led to a radical transformation of the city's appearance, in which whole districts were destroyed or remodelled or rebuilt. Sanitization of the city, which was treated as a priority, began with the enormous task of covering the River Senne and the installation of a sewerage system; this was followed by the clearing of what would become Brussels' central boulevards. Linking the Gare du Nord to the new Gare du Midi, these were inaugurated in 1871 and lined on either side by many public buildings, theatres, covered passages, cafés and shops. The new streets joined one another at wide squares embellished with sculptures erected for both decorative and educational reasons, with the purpose of appealing to the patriotism of the inhabitants as well as satisfying bourgeois taste.

View of the Mont des Arts, Brussels
Postcard
Private collection

The law courts, Brussels
Postcard
Private collection

ELLES *La Place Royale*

Place Royale, Brussels
Postcard
Private collection

In addition to the remodelling of the city centre. Brussels was extended eastwards with rectilinear avenues creating the grid of the new Léopold district where the upper middle class settled. Also laid down in an easterly direction, the Rue de la Loi and the Rue du Trône, as well as the Avenue Louise led towards the Bois de la Cambre, which was much appreciated by the population due to the city's lack of green spaces. The king took a personal and active interest, to the extent of sometimes contributing financially, in the different projects that instated long and broad views and public parks to instil a sense of openness, for example, with the creation of the park and the Palais du Cinquantenaire to hold the national jubilee exhibition in 1880. This site – with the two buildings that would later become the army and air force museums, linked by a semicircular colonnade and a triumphal arch – would also be used to accommodate the Universal Exposition in 1897. Many other spaces in the city were used for building projects, some accompanied by disagreement, as occurred between the king and burgomaster of Brussels with regard to the development of the lower section of the Montagne de la Cour – the future 'Mont des Arts' where today the Bibliothèque Royale, the Musée des Beaux-Arts and the Archives stand – over the decision whether or not to demolish a Renaissance district: in the end it was destroyed.

Of all the monumental building projects of the period, the largest was unquestionably that of the law courts designed by Joseph Poelaert, construction of which lasted between 1866 and 1883. This imposing building, which overlooks the city, was largely approved of and its enormous size considered an appropriate reflec-

Place de Brouckère, Brussels
Postcard
Private collection

tion of the greatness of the Belgian nation. Other law courts, also very large, were built during the same period in Ghent and Antwerp. The style of both public and private buildings in Brussels and elsewhere manifested the triumph of historicism: architects were inspired by a real or imaginary past and drew on classical antiquity, Gothic and baroque architecture, and heavily from the Flemish Neo-Renaissance for reasons of nationalist pride. The facades were often a mixture of these styles, assimilated with varying degrees of success. It was at this time that the tendency began to arise among certain artists, towards the end of the century, to shrug off traditional standards and invent an *'art nouveau'*.

One of the important consequences of the renovation of Brussels was the banishment of the humbler levels of the population to the outskirts: the workers were relegated to the industrial districts in the west, while the affluent classes resided in the east. It was this rich bourgeoisie, proud of its values, that governed the country, and it was to them that the capital offered its pleasures, concerts and plays. But these prosperous years also marked the birth of an educated generation of lower-middle-class inhabitants who felt their lack of political influence – the voting system was still based on the poll tax – and demanded a voice. This social setting was the origin of many intellectuals and artists who met in the city cafés, debated the social conditions and wished to express their feelings on the situation. Concurrently, at the end of the 1870s, the country began to head towards a serious economic crisis that was to alter the power relationships in Belgian society acutely.

A new vision

vision

Matter revealed

REALISM
THE SOCIÉTÉ LIBRE
DES BEAUX-ARTS

"To produce wholesome, strong, original painting; to return to the true meaning of the painting, loved not for the sake of the subject but for its own rich materiality, as both precious substance and living organism; to paint nature in its reality, its frankness, its accent, detached from known masteries and systems."

In 1848, the year known as the "Springtime of the Peoples", the wave of rebellion that flowed across Europe had no immediate political consequences in Belgium. In this young country, preoccupied with winning a place for itself in the banqueting table of the nations, social protest was not an issue. Bourgeois capitalism was the rule of the day and, even if dissatisfaction with the system was not non-existent, it was still disorganized and unguided.

However, everyone could see, especially among the growing intellectual class, that the values established in the 1830s were no longer valid and did not coincide with the circumstances of the moment. When Belgium's neighbouring countries demanded to become egalitarian republics, how was it possible to continue accepting suffrage on the basis of property qualifications, and to allow capitalism alone to direct the country's politics? Was it possible to deny the existence of poverty and

social conditions? And, in the arts, at the time that Delacroix was revolutionizing painting in France and Courbet was painting his *Stone-Breakers*, which was exhibited in Brussels in 1851, wasn't it imperative to break away from the past, with all its romantic mists and frozen conventions? In the middle of the century, these questions were passionately debated in artistic and literary circles by a young generation loudly laying claim to freedom: the freedom to describe reality and the freedom for all to speak their minds. Some of the painters who voiced their protest were Félicien Rops, Louis Artan, Charles de Groux, Constantin Meunier and Camille van Camp.

Freedom of expression was exactly what the Société Libre des Beaux-Arts, founded in 1868, set as its goal in its inaugural manifesto drafted by Camille van Camp: "Without disdaining the immense services rendered by tradition, which is taken as our frame of reference, the society knows no other point of departure for artistic evolution than the one from which the renewal of art has always ensued. That is to say the free and individual interpretation of nature." Some twenty painters, of which a few had already made a name for themselves, announced publicly and jointly their refusal to accept the decisions made by the panel of the Salon, the restrictive rules of academicism and all pictorial conventions, so that they could return to focusing

EDMOND LAMBRICHS, **Portrait of the Members of the Société Libre des Beaux-Arts**, *undated*
Oil on canvas, 175 × 236 cm
Inv. 3352

The Société Libre des Beaux-Arts was founded in 1868 with the aim of defending realist painting and the freedom of the artist. This painting of its members includes many landscape artists: from left to right, seated, Édouard Huberti, F. Boudin, Charles de Groux, Camille van Camp, Antoine-Félix Bouré, Alfred Verwée, Constantin Meunier, Louis Dubois (holding a copy of *L'Art libre* and *L'Art universel*); standing, Edmond Lambrichs, Louis Artan, Félicien Rops, Jules Raeymaeckers, Jean-Baptiste Meunier, Eugène Smits, Théodore Baron, Hippolyte de la Charlerie.

CHARLES HERMANS, At Dawn, *1875*
Oil on canvas, 248 × 317 cm
Inv. 2812

This painting caused a sensation at the Salon de Bruxelles in 1875.
On the left we see a few clean and dignified members of the working
class looking reprovingly at representatives of bourgeois society
leaving a place of pleasure at dawn. The man in a fur coat at the door
seems to be aware of this social confrontation, while the drunken
man and the two women hanging onto him seem to be headed for
the gutter and the rubbish lying in it. The combination of the social
subject and the work's outsize format, usually reserved for history
paintings, caused *At Dawn* to be thought of as a manifesto of realism.

ALFRED STEVENS, **Autumn Flowers**, *1867*
Oil on canvas, 74.5 × 55 cm
Inv. 3526

Influenced at the start of his career by Flemish painting.
Alfred Stevens (1823–1906) painted personal, domestic scenes
then veered towards realism by focusing on the lives of the
humble and poor. But he achieved fame and honours more for
his many paintings of elegant women in their personal settings.
in which Stevens demonstrated his remarkable qualities as
a colourist and the importance he placed on painterly skills.

on the truthfulness of their perceptions of the real world and thus create a new form of painting. In *L'École belge de peinture (1830-1905)*, written in 1906, the author Camille Lemonnier summed up the aim of these painters in a single sentence that became famous: "To produce wholesome, strong, original painting; to return to the true meaning of the painting, loved not for the sake of the subject but for its own rich materiality, as both precious substance and living organism; to paint nature in its reality, its frankness, its accent, detached from known masteries and systems." The Société Libre des Beaux-Arts organized its own exhibitions for eight years and finally won the battle when the doors of the Salons were opened to realists. In 1875 some of the members of the society had joined another association of painters, La Chrysalide, which would exhibit the works of James Ensor.

The founders and sympathizers of the Société Libre des Beaux-Arts were not unknown to one another. Many had studied and trained together, for example, the fairly bohemian teachings at the Saint-Luc studio at the start of the 1850s, where Félicien Rops, Louis Artan and Constantin Meunier had met. At that time they were already seeking their own directions and discussing painting and literature as the dialogue between artists and writers was one that had been constant.

One of the painters who militated at that time for freedom of thought was Rops, whose rebellious spirit showed itself very early. Having entered the Université Libre de Bruxelles in 1851 when he was eighteen, he quickly found a place among the most active students and was a member of the Société des Joyeux, where he made friends with the writer Charles de Coster, its principal spokesman. Together they created the review *Uylenspiegel. Journal des ébats artistiques et littéraires*, which argued vociferously in defence of realism and naturalism. Next, Rops engraved plates for de Coster's books, *Légendes flamandes, Contes brabançons* and, most importantly,

La Légende et les aventures d'Ulenspiegel et de Lamme Goedzack (1867), in which the author revisited local traditions in search of the Flemish genius. This cultural substrate was later agreed by all intellectuals and artists to be the origin of Belgian realism. The new ideas were diffused by the growing number of reviews, of which the most important were *L'Art libre* (1871-72), *L'Art universel* (1873-75) and *L'Artiste* (1875-80): their articles, those by Camille Lemonnier in particular, laid claim to a Belgian "naturalist tradition" in both painting and literature, and also to modernity, by which he meant awareness and appreciation of the truth of reality.

Not all the artists understood this truth in the same manner. Some searched for it in nature, like Louis Artan, a painter of the sea and the light, who attempted to capture the transience of atmosphere; another was Hippolyte Boulenger, who founded a colony in the forest of Tervueren, in an attempt to create a likeness of the Barbizon School of which Daubigny, Corot and Rousseau were members; and lastly Louis Dubois, who worked in all the painting genres and focused his attention on working the pictorial matter – what he admired most in Corot, as he wrote in *L'Art libre*. Others chose domestic interiors, such as Henri de Braekeleer and, in a different manner, Alfred Stevens, "the most Parisian of the Belgian painters", who portrayed women in their refined, bourgeois settings.

In the field of genre scenes, *At Dawn* by Charles Hermans is a prodigious example of realist painting: in its very contemporary subject and size, which are those of a history painting, and in its message, which is clearly a social criticism. He was one of the first in a long line of painters who, until the end of the century, would depict social themes.

CHARLES VAN DER STAPPEN,
The Man with a Sword, *1876-79*
Statue, marble and bronze,
186.5 × 101.5 × 89.5 cm
Inv. 2805

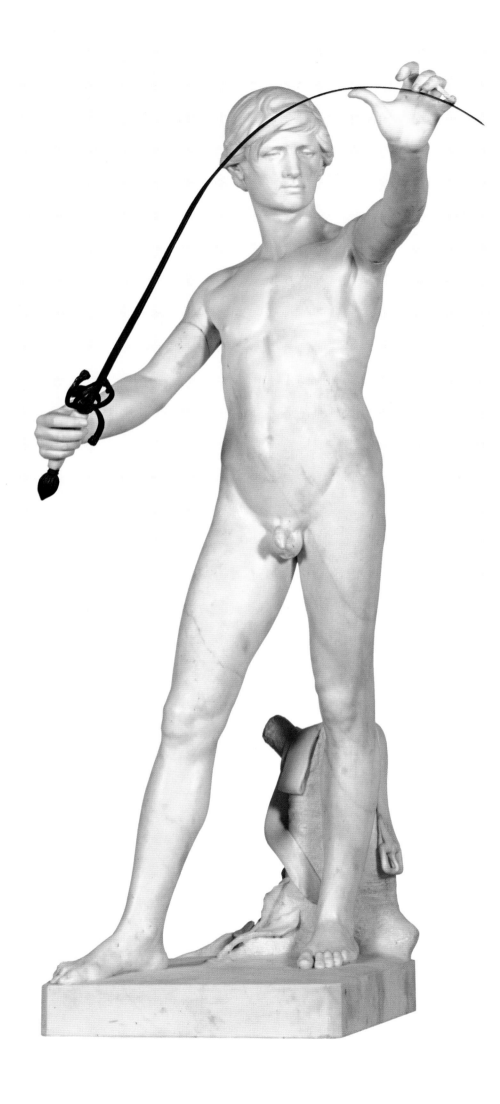

LOUIS DUBOIS, Storks, *1858*
Oil on canvas, 153 × 277 cm
Inv. 2807

Louis Dubois (1830–1880) was a pupil at the Atelier Libre Saint-Luc
at the same time as Rops, Artan and Meunier. He was again at their
side in the Société Libre des Beaux-Arts, of which he was a very active
member, in particular taking up his pen to defend the realism of Courbet
in *L'Art libre*. An artist who considered the skills of the painter's trade
very important, he left a varied production, including landscapes, still lifes,
portraits and genre scenes. His *Storks* is bathed in an atmosphere
of mystery that heralded symbolism.

LOUIS ARTAN DE SAINT-MARTIN, The Wreck, *1871*
Oil on canvas mounted on panel, 142 × 248 cm
Inv. 2971

Louis Artan's encounter with the masters of French realism, Courbet
and Corot, during a visit to Paris led Louis Artan (1837–1890) to
focus his attention on the effects of the light. Following a stay in
Brittany, he understood that his vocation was to paint the sea, so he
moved to the coast in Belgium and dedicated himself to depicting
seascapes in which he attempted to pin down fleeting atmospheric
effects and the shimmering of the water. The French impressionists
were attempting to do exactly the same thing at that very moment.

HIPPOLYTE BOULENGER, **The Alley of Old Hornbeams, Tervueren,**
1871–72
Oil on canvas, 130.5 × 93 cm
Inv. 2632

Boulenger (1837–1874) took up plein-air landscape painting in Tervueren,
near Brussels, where several painters had already installed themselves.
In 1866 he gave the group the name of 'School of Tervueren',
a somewhat ironic title but one that would later prevail. However, the
parallel he attempted to create with the French Barbizon School did
not lack sense as Boulenger, too, extolled a true art in direct contact
with nature. As a painter his tools were the matter and his instinct,
and his style evolved towards a certain expressionism. Close to
the Société Libre des Beaux-Arts, Boulenger played a significant
role in the development of Belgian landscape painting.

HENRI DE BRAEKELEER, **The Man at the Window,** c. *1873–76*
Oil on canvas, 80.5 × 70 cm
Inv. 3857

Born into a family of painters, Henri de Braekeleer (1840–1888)
received a meticulous training, which explains his precision and
sense of detail. After painting the common people, he made
a speciality of indoor scenes, often in the Dutch tradition
of the seventeenth century. Solitary and suffering from
mental illness, he had a fairly chaotic career.

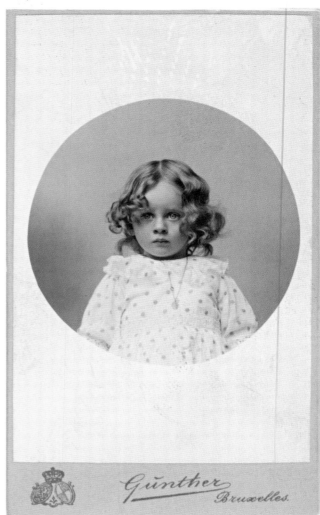

Günther
Bruxelles

Erinnerung an den

→ Drachenfels. ←

PHOTOGRAPHY

"The merciless objectivity of photography, which was often scorned by artists, did nothing to prevent a general fascination for these new images in which the middle classes of all countries could admire themselves."

Photography's close relationship with painting, and more generally with art, has been analysed since its inception as it offered a completely new way of representing reality. The scrutiny continued to broaden and deepen as photography became more technically and financially accessible to the public at large. There was little in common between the first, individual photographs on tin by Nicéphore Niépce and the economically priced pictures made possible by George Eastman's instant camera sold by Kodak in 1888. Sixty years were required to achieve this progress in the manipulation of images, during which time the artistic aspect of photography was continually debated. One of the practical responses to the question was pictorialism, a style of photography created in the 1880s by artists who used and worked with different photographic processes with the aim of producing a genuine work of art (see box, p. 35). In parallel, a large number of poets and writers theorized the characteristics of the photographic image, refusing to restrict it to a simple reproduction of reality and wishing to make it a facet of aesthetic, even symbolic creation – a view expressed by Maurice Maeterlinck in the second issue of *Camera Work* (1903) in an article about the photographer Edward Steichen.

Many of the portraits exhibited in this museum retrace the technical developments made up until the start of the twentieth century, starting from the daguerreotype invented at the beginning of colour photography. Patented in 1839 by its inventor, Louis Daguerre, the daguerreotype was one of the first processes that made it possible to record an image permanently, though not yet to reproduce it. The technique relied on the use of a camera obscura in which the image was printed on a copper plate faced with silver and made light sensitive by the fumes of iodine crystals. The exposure time was no longer up to ten hours, as required by Niépce's process, but between twenty and thirty minutes, which was later reduced to just a few dozen seconds. The accuracy and quality of the images fired the public with enthusiasm and the piece of equipment to capture them sold so well that the term 'daguerreotypomania' was coined. However, Daguerre's image-making process was soon rivalled by the calotype, invented by the Englishman William Henry Fox Talbot, which gave a negative of the image and thus allowed an unlimited number of prints to be made of it. Other processes followed, such as the ambrotype on a glass plate and the ferrotype on a chemically treated metal plate, which

ANONYMOUS, Portrait of a Woman, c. *1860*
Framed ambrotype, 25.7 × 21.5 cm
Musées Royaux d'Art et d'Histoire, Brussels
Inv. PH 0000420

GHUNTHER *(Brussels)*, Portrait of a Young Child,
undated
Platen print (visiting card), 10.4 × 6.2 cm
Musées Royaux d'Art et d'Histoire, Brussels
Inv. PH 0000461

PERRAUD *(Lyon, France)*, Portrait of a Man,
undated
Framed daguerreotype, 28.5 × 24.5 cm
Musées Royaux d'Art et d'Histoire, Brussels
Inv. PH 0003698

ANONYMOUS, Group Portrait, *15 May 1901*
Inscription recto: Erinnerung an den Drachenfels
Inscription verso: C. Dangotten Johanna Breidenback,
Hedwig Halbach, Hermine Büekl, Lydia Bencker,
Anne-Marie Maïjer, Irma Thom
Dimensions with frame, 12 × 10 cm
Ferrotype
Musées Royaux d'Art et d'Histoire, Brussels
Inv. PH 0001593

ALEXANDRE, Two Tigers in a Cage (Antwerp Zoo),
undated
Gelatin silver bromide transparency on glass,
8.5 × 10 cm
Musées Royaux d'Art et d'Histoire, Brussels
Inv. PH 0010013

contributed to the falling expense and increasing speed of photographic reproduction. The limited cost of some processes coupled with the invention of apparatus that could use several lenses was to lead, for example, to the manufacture of image-based visiting cards, a vogue that, it is said, made its inventor a millionaire.

Painters quickly came to view photography as heralding the end of their source of income. Beginning in the 1840s, many of them took an interest in the new field to the point of becoming professional photographers themselves. In their studios, like in those of photographers from different backgrounds, their models were placed in 'artistic' settings of carefully placed furniture, draped curtains and personalized accessories. Some photographers offered to take their equipment to the home of their clients or in their garden to take individual or group portraits. The merciless objectivity of photography, which was often scorned by artists, did nothing to prevent a general fascination for these new images in which the middle classes of all countries could admire themselves.

Initially the preserve of the better-off, photography became progressively available to all and, when it relinquished the studios, offered everyone the possibility of magically capturing images of faces and places. 'You press the button, we do the rest,' claimed Kodak in its advertising. In an effort to fight against the standardization of images that these technical developments had made possible, some amateur photographers strove to defend a certain photographic aesthetic in the conviction that photography was a wholly artistic practice. This gave rise, after the founding of the first professional photographers' societies, to the creation

throughout Europe of the first, very active, amateur photographers' associations. The Association Belge de Photographie (ABP) was founded in 1873, accompanied by the publication of a *Bulletin* giving information and news through its local sections, the quality of which brought it recognition beyond the country's borders. Each year the association held an international salon that enabled the work of different countries to be compared. In 1892 the ABP presented some 270 images, most of which were the work of British photographers. The exhibition made a strong impression and showed the public that, according to the organizers, 'photography has to be considered an art'.

This claim was intensified with the invention in 1903 of the autochrome by Louis and Auguste Lumière. This technique for the creation of colour pictures was rather complicated as it required – once the shot had been set up – a glass plate on which a sprinkling of grains of potato starch dyed orange, violet and green was fixed by resin, with the spaces between the grains filled by lampblack. Exposure and the two-part development process were equally complex, but in spite of these difficulties, or perhaps because it was not just a question of instant photos available to one and all, many amateur and professional photographers eagerly took up the new process. And it was thus that colour photographs were taken of the events of the First World War, photojournalistic reportages across the world and botanical images, just to mention the documentary contribution of the autochrome. Its success continued until 1935 when the development of Kodachrome film progressively replaced it. Restricted to black and white throughout the nineteenth century, photographers could finally take advantage of the full visible colour range. Colour not only injected a 'surplus' of truth into photographic representations, it facilitated unprecedented artistic views. Often taking their inspiration from painters, 'autochromists' experimented with the relationship between colours, and variations in the light and its limpidity, nuances that black-and-white images could not match. With this advance, photography joined the ranks of the fine arts.

ANONYMOUS, Portrait of a Lady, c. *1915*
Gelatin silver bromide negative on glass,
18 × 13 cm
Musées royaux d'Art et d'Histoire, Brussels
Inv. PH 0000835

PICTORIALISM

To counter the standardization of images resulting from technical progress, some amateur photographers developed an aesthetic in which emphasis was placed on the sensibility of the artist-photographer. This led, between 1890 and 1914, to pictorialism, which was applied equally to landscapes, portraits and pictures of buildings. It employed a variety of techniques to transform the representation of reality, such as blurring or fuzziness, chiaroscuro, cropped framing and manually intervening on the negative. The great names of pictorialism are Robert Demachy, the figurehead of French pictorialism, the American Alvin Coburn and, above all, Edward Steichen (1879–1973), who assimilated artistic influences from both Europe and the United States. From 1890 many associations held photographic exhibitions, such as the camera clubs of Paris and Vienna. After 1900 pictorialism radiated internationally due, in particular, to Alfred Stieglitz (1864–1946), who founded the Photo-Secession and its accompanying magazine *Camera Work*. His gallery in New York exhibited photographic works by pictorialists, as well as avant-garde art from Europe, notably by Rodin, Matisse and Picasso.

HECTOR COLLARD, Light Rays and Shadows, *1895*
Gum bichromate on paper, 26 × 36.3 cm
(with original frame: 41.8 × 52.9 cm)
Musées Royaux d'Art et d'Histoire, Brussels
Alg. inv. 7317 – PH 0000006

LÉONARD MISONNE, Dusty Path, *1898*
Gelatin silver print, 29.8 × 38.5 cm
(with original frame: 61.8 × 75.9 cm)
Musées Royaux d'Art et d'Histoire, Brussels
Inv. PH 0000022

SOCIAL REALISM
THE ECONOMIC CRISIS
AND THE SOCIAL QUESTION

"Meanwhile, a wave of sympathy for the suffering working class arose among the circles of libertarian artists."

VINCENT VAN GOGH, The Peasant, *1885*
Oil on canvas, 39 × 30.5 cm
Inv. 4910

Still uncertain of his vocation as a painter, and having become a lay preacher, Vincent van Gogh (1853-1890) was posted to an evangelical mission in the Borinage, where he lived between 1878 and 1880. He witnessed the poverty of the miners and farmworkers, whose living conditions he voluntarily shared and who inspired him to produce a series of pathos-filled works.

From 1848, authors and artists shifted their attention to the description of real life in both painting and literature. Over the decades that followed, with life in constant change and the economic crisis that arose in Belgium in 1874 having a profound effect on the social situation, they continued to treat this subject matter but using different forms. The rapid development of the country since it gained independence was abruptly interrupted with the outbreak of the Franco-Prussian War in 1870 due to the closure of the markets and thus the halting of orders from the United States, which had till then been a large importer of coal and steel. In an economy in which foreign markets and customers were fundamental, the consequences were dramatic. Furthermore, the Americans were selling huge quantities of wheat to Belgium, thus making large numbers of agricultural labourers redundant; in consequence, these men looked for work in factories but industry was unable to absorb them all. These developments marked the start of a long recession accompanied by social

misery and justified revolts. The crisis came to a head in 1884-85 with worker demonstrations that troops were brought in to quell, resulting in bloody confrontations that caused fear among politicians who had until that moment been little aware of the extent of the social menace. Meanwhile, a wave of sympathy for the suffering working class arose among the circles of libertarian artists. The poet Émile Verhaeren, the progressive intellectual Edmond Picard and painters like Ensor and Toorop publicly voiced their espousal of social causes, and soon many intellectuals and artists pledged their support to the Belgian Workers' Party, created in 1885 to fight for universal suffrage.

The literary world documented the social developments in its own way. Camille Lemonnier used magazine articles to lead the campaign of support for Émile Zola, in particular with regard to his novel *Germinal*; the fact that this support was offered in parallel with that of French authors led to the establishment of relations between Brussels and Paris, which remained close during the fin-de-siècle period. Lemonnier was also the author of the first Belgian naturalist novel, *Un mâle*, whose fierceness made an impression on the public. The other great naturalist novelist of the period was Georges Eekhoud whose

CONSTANTIN MEUNIER,
The Broken Crucible, *1885*
Oil on canvas, 160.5 × 303 cm
Inv. 10.000/233

In the glassmaking industry, a crucible is the container that holds the molten material after it has been removed from the furnace. As it is raised to very high temperatures, the crucible often breaks and needs to be replaced. This scene, which Constantin Meunier (1831-1905) witnessed in Val Saint-Lambert, is a powerful representation, in a magnificent composition, of the moment the workers jointly remove the crucible in what we can imagine is quite blistering heat.

La Nouvelle Carthage (1888) painted a portrait of society that contained a damning critique of capitalism. In pages that became famous, he described the living conditions of workers affected by pollution, their powerlessness and spirit, and the despair of families forced by poverty to emigrate to America.

The writings of Georges Eekhoud were a strong influence on painters, in particular Eugène Laermans, who drew his subjects from the worlds of the industrial worker and agricultural labourer. His pessimistic vision and deep pathos made him a defender of the social causes of his time but, more broadly, his concern was to illustrate the fragility of the human condition. Throughout his career he gave his oeuvre greater relevance and application by stripping it of all unnecessary detail. In bestowing greater significance on the purely aesthetic aspects of his images, he opened the way to Flemish expressionism.

The common people were also the focus of the oeuvre of Léon Frederic. He painted realist scenes of the rural men and women of Flanders and the factory workers of the Ardennes in natural settings that are themselves very present. Frederic evoked these same people in his later works through allegory. However, the dignity of work found a very eloquent apostle in Constantin Meunier: in particular, this outstanding painter and sculptor produced the sculpture *Firedamp*, in which a woman bends over the body of a child killed by the invisible and odourless gas that seeps up from the coal deposits, and *The Puddler*, the powerful figure of a metalworker, described as a sort of 'David of the industrial era'. It was when he discovered the coal-mining area of the Borinage in 1878 that Meunier became aware of the world associated with industrial production and he immediately grasped its grandeur and harshness. 'He opened art to [the subject of] all those fearful people hiding in the shadows', as Camille Lemonnier was to comment. However, Constantin Meunier's production goes much further than the defence of the more vulnerable ranks of society to express humanity's eternal emotional nature.

EUGÈNE LAERMANS, **The Evening of the Strike,** *1893*
Oil on canvas, 106 × 115 cm
Inv. 4681

When Eugène Laermans (1864–1940) painted this canvas in 1893, social tension in Belgium was at its peak. Throngs of workers from factories and the countryside flowed into the cities, creating scenes that struck the artist forcefully and which he painted on several occasions. Here he shows a dense, anonymous, though visibly determined crowd carrying a red flag against a background of factories with smoking chimneys.

LÉON FREDERIC, **The Chalk Sellers.** *Left wing:* Morning. *Centre:* Midday.
Right wing: Evening, *1882–83*
Oil on canvas, 200 × 267.5 cm (central panel), 200 × 115 cm (wings)
Inv. 3263

Frequent in the Middle Ages and Renaissance. the triptych came back
into fashion in the late nineteenth century among the Nazarenes in
Germany and the Pre-Raphaelites in England. as well as in Belgium.
Léon Frederic (1856–1940) painted some sixty polyptychs, a format he
considered suitable to present the issues of the moment to the public.
Here he shows three moments in the life of a family of peddlers:
setting out at daybreak, the pause for their frugal midday meal,
and their return home in the evening. He succeeds in his sympathetic
depiction of the apprehensiveness of the children, whose resignation
and fortitude in performing their duties can be clearly discerned.

CONSTANTIN MEUNIER, The Puddler, *1884–87/88*
Seated statue, bronze, 145.5 × 81.5 × 87.5 cm
Inv. 3066

A puddler was a metalworker whose role was to roll the molten metal into a
lump, then to extract it from the furnace and transfer it to the hammermen.
As the job required great physical strength, it was reserved for powerful
men, like the one Constantin Meunier has portrayed here.
We see the puddler during his pause: his hanging arm still holds the
puddling bar, and his haggard face and slumped shoulders reveal
his immense fatigue after the effort he has just made.

CONSTANTIN MEUNIER, Firedamp: Woman Finding
Her Son Among the Dead, *1889*
Group, bronze, 151.5 × 212 × 108.5 cm
Inv. 3200

THE CONSTANTIN MEUNIER MUSEUM

Located in the house-cum-studio that Meunier had built for himself in the Rue de l'Abbaye, Ixelles, in 1899, the Constantin Meunier Museum was opened to the public in 1939 and incorporated into the Musées royaux des Beaux-Arts in Brussels in 1978. It holds some 150 works created between 1880 and 1905, the period that the artist considered his 'second life', in which he engaged in social commentary. His realist paintings and drawings show the world of work, such as *The Broken Crucible* (1885), executed after his encounter with the industrial region of the Liège basin. There he witnessed both the suffering and destitution of the workers and the remarkable power of industrial production at that time. The museum also exhibits works executed by Meunier after his return to sculpture that had a strong effect on realist art: plaster and bronze works, sometimes of large format, that pay tribute to the miners, metalworkers and farmworkers who were the anonymous heroes of modern progress.

The fascination of light

An explosion of colour

JAMES ENSOR

"Ensor's trajectory fell perfectly within the artistic trends of the fin de siècle as he passed from realism to the subjective expression of his inner experiences."

James Ensor's talent showed itself so early that at the age of fifteen he was already painting small views of the surroundings of Ostend, his home town, with great feeling. Although the formal teaching he received between 1877 and 1880 at the Académie Royale des Beaux-Arts in Brussels was scarcely suited to his rebellious nature, he profited from these three years to study the works of the great masters Hals, Rembrandt and Goya, as well as more recent artists like Turner and Manet, from engravings. On his return to Ostend, which he would not leave for the rest of his life, he painted landscapes, interiors and still lifes characterized by dark colours and thick matter often worked with a palette knife. His so-called 'light' period that followed focused mostly on the expression of light and the use of pure colour, and repeatedly employed such motifs as masks and skeletons. From that moment on Ensor's output shifted away from imitative representation to encompass an 'esthétique de l'étrange' that has similarities with the oeuvre of the future surrealists.

His technique and imaginative universe were so idiosyncratic that Ensor had great difficulty in getting his works exhibited. He was finally embraced by certain avant-garde circles like La Chrysalide and L'Essor (1881 and 1882) and, although he had been a founder-member of Les XX, the works he sent were only accepted grudgingly by the group despite friendly support from some members, such as Émile Verhaeren.

His satirical outlook and refusal to compromise annoyed his fellow-artists, to the point that his important painting *The Entry of Christ into Brussels in 1889* (1888) was refused by Les XX. 'In 1890, a new cabal. Reactionary opposition, and certain malicious peers voted against', Ensor related years later. Misunderstood by critics and feeling wounded, he should have left Les XX but its Salons were the only way to get his work known by the public. He thus remained a member in spite of the real, or supposed, hostility of the group until it was dissolved in 1893.

Around 1900, Ensor's creative mettle seemed to dim and, though he continued to work shut up in his house in Ostend surrounded by masks, shells and exotic souvenirs, he was content to recycle the themes of his younger years. However, he spent more time on writing and dreamed about being a composer. Then, little by little with the passing of the years, the recognition he had long awaited began to arrive: he received enthusiastic visitors, leading museums bought and exhibited his works, and in 1929 the Belgian king made him a baron while an important retrospective of his oeuvre was being held in the Palais des Beaux-Arts in Brussels.

Ensor's trajectory fell perfectly within the artistic trends of the fin de siècle as he passed from realism to the subjective expression of his inner experiences. His feverish preoccupation with light, whose mystical aspect he glorified, linked him with symbolism, a connection corroborated by the recurrence of certain

JAMES ENSOR, **Russian Music**, *1881*
Oil on canvas, 133 × 110 cm
Inv. 4679

Russian Music is one of a set of oppressive, muffled, middle-class interiors that Ensor (1860-1949) painted in the early 1880s. It is from the artist's 'dark' period, in which he worked a soft impasto with a palette knife. The setting is a family drawing room, with curios suggestive of the exotic objects that his parents used to trade. Two years after this work was completed, Fernand Khnopff painted the very similar *Listening to Schumann* (p. 103); convinced that he had been plagiarized by his colleague at Les XX, Ensor broke with him.

James Ensor in his studio-living room in Ostend, 1927
Black and white photograph (contact print),
13.4 × 23.7 cm. Inv. AACB 8093

themes, such as masks, skeletons and Christ, with whom he frequently identified. It was not long before his use of masks, at first anecdotal, was transformed into his vision of mankind – ridiculous yet terrifying puppets: to him they were more than a form of entertainment, they were the means to hide one's true self and to distort reality, but also to authorize all liberties: unmoving and silent, they make it possible to express our most secret fantasies. As for skeletons, which are representative of the painter's ceaseless obsession with death, they are sometimes represented as demons, and sometimes as caricatures in satirical paintings that mock art critics, doctors, policemen and anyone linked with institutional life.

But if there is one genre that James Ensor never turned his back, it was landscape painting, in which he gave the full measure of his qualities as a luminist and painter of matter. Like Constable, Turner and Courbet, some of the artists he had chosen as his masters,

JAMES ENSOR, **Skeletons Fighting Over a Smoked Herring,** *1891*
Oil on panel, 16 × 21.5 cm
Inv. 11156

Two skeletons, one of whom is wearing a policeman's hat of the period, are tugging on a smoked herring with their teeth. The painting is a clear visual allusion to the play on words Ensor = art-Ensor (the French word for smoked herring is hareng saur, with a similar pronunciation to 'art-Ensor'), a deprecatory term that had been flung at the painter in 1885, but which he had taken with good humour and used on several occasions by representing himself as a fish. The strangely dramatic atmosphere is created by the two macabre figures but also by the ferocity with which they are fighting over their miserable prize, which has been torn by their vicious teeth. The skeletons are evidently a metaphor for art critics, a clique detested by Ensor, who considered himself their victim.

Ensor was not content to create an illusionistic rendition of a cloudy sky: at a more fundamental level, he attempted to express the idea of a cloudy sky through the substance itself of the paint on the canvas. This was exactly the same principle on which the expressionists were later to base their own approach.

JAMES ENSOR, The Bad Doctors, *1892*
Oil on panel, 50 × 61 cm
Université Libre de Bruxelles, Brussels

∧ JAMES ENSOR, **The Drunkards**, *1883*
Oil on canvas, 115 × 165 cm
Belfius Banque Collection, Brussels
Inv. 1591

< JAMES ENSOR, **The Lamp-Lighter**, *1880*
Oil on canvas, 151.5 × 91 cm
Inv. 3294

Page 52: JAMES ENSOR, **The Scandalized Masks**, *1883* >>
Oil on canvas, 135 × 112 cm
Inv. 4190

Page 53: JAMES ENSOR, **Strange Masks**, *1892*
Oil on canvas, 100 × 80 cm
Inv. 4194

Ensor first included masks in his work in 1883, in the painting titled *The Scandalized Masks*. In this work painted ten years later, the masked figures have increased in number to create a carnival scene. The vivid colours represent the exhilaration of the event and are suffused with a beautiful, strong light, something Ensor always sought out: 'light is my daughter', 'light, the painter's bread', he used to say. The painting also presents a vision of the world, with bodiless figures who conceal their dramas. In this work, 'ideal and matter, reality and imagination march arm-in-arm towards a patch of horizon', in the words of the artist.

JAMES ENSOR, Ostend Lighthouse, *1885*
Oil on canvas, 62 × 75 cm
Inv. 4866

à mon ami C.
Déc. 85

LES XX
LA LIBRE ESTHÉTIQUE

"What I like extraordinarily in Les XX
is their absence of a programme.
A programme is already a rule.
Rules are 'methodist'. Method
and doctrine are sisters."

The ferment of ideas and creative fervour for which Brussels was the setting at the start of the 1880s were reflected in the publication of twenty or so new reviews, of which the most important would be *L'Art moderne* (1881-1914), started by Octave Maus, Edmond Picard and Eugène Robert, and *La Jeune Belgique* (1881-97). Founded by a group of poets and writers that included Georges Rodenbach, Émile Verhaeren, Max Waller and Albert Giraud, *La Jeune Belgique* attracted the leading representatives of the most modern trends of the moment – symbolist poets and naturalist novelists – but also French poets like Verlaine and Mallarmé. Particularly dynamic, these two reviews organized numerous events and agitated for a rapprochement of the arts.

Another characteristic of the era was the creation of circles and alternative exhibition spaces, following the example of the Société Libre des Beaux-Arts in 1868. Less than ten years later, in 1876, the association L'Essor was established, which had as its motto, '*Un art unique, une vie unique*' (A unique art, one life), to emphasize the link that exists between art and life. The founders, who were considered progressives, were soon joined by artists such as Fernand Khnopff, who first participated in one of their exhibitions in 1881, James Ensor, Théo van Rysselberghe, Guillaume Vogels and Léon Frederic, to mention only the names that posterity has retained. But dissension soon arose between its members,

with some reproaching not only the fact it had no programme, but also its lack of discrimination, in that it accepted traditional realists as well as the avant-garde as members.

Thus Khnopff, Ensor, van Rysselberghe, Vogels and Frederic resigned from L'Essor in 1883 and joined an association of artists being set up that would be called Les XX, the name reflecting the fact that they indeed numbered about twenty. Octave Maus, one of the founders of *L'Art moderne*, became its secretary. The purpose of the association was defined during its first meeting, held at the Taverne Guillaume in the Place du Musée in Brussels: to fight 'for the defence of an intransigent art' and to represent 'the conscious and organized insurrection against academicism'.

'What I like extraordinarily in Les XX is their absence of a programme. A programme is already a rule. Rules are 'methodist'. Method and doctrine are sisters.' These are the words used by Félicien Rops to explain why he was accepting the invitation from Les XX to show his work at its first exhibition. The innovative aspect of the way Les XX operated lay in its having suppressed all notion of rank and having no panel of judges. Equality between the artists was advocated, and the absence of hierarchy and dogma was an ideal not unconnected with the anarchist currents extant at the time. Rules were, however, drawn up to regulate the group's exhibitions: the *vingtistes* would invite twenty other artists to exhibit with them; each *vingtiste* would have the right to exhibit six works and guests one; the group's exhibition would be annual and held in February.

THÉO VAN RYSSELBERGHE, **Portrait of Octave Maus,** *1885*
Oil on canvas, 90.5 × 75.5 cm
Inv. 6383

A lawyer, writer and art critic, Octave Maus (1856-1919) was one of the three founders of *L'Art moderne*. The secretary of Les XX, then director of La Libre Esthétique, he showed himself to be an ardent defender of modernity in the exhibitions, lectures and concerts he organized. A Wagner lover from the start, he was one of the pilgrims who travelled to Bayreuth and later became a member of the Wagner society in Brussels.

Announced several weeks in advance in *L'Art moderne*, the first Salon des XX opened at the Palais des Beaux-Arts in Brussels on 1 February 1884 and was reviewed by *Émile* Verhaeren in *La Jeune Belgique* in glowing terms: 'These are the select {artists} of the young {generation.} . . . Their works confirm that they are guided by conquering boldness, solicited by the desire to discover the new, fortified by determination . . . They are in no way imitators, they simply work like all non-reactionary artists work today, breathing in the atmosphere of the age, outside of which it would be madness to search for air.' The exhibitors included foreign guests: Rodin from France, Mauve and Israels from Holland, Whistler from England despite his American origin, Liebermann from Germany and Sargent from the United States. Other foreign artists would be present at later exhibitions, chosen 'among artists already established, but whose art remains independent and combative', such as Pissarro, Monet, Seurat, Gauguin, Cézanne and van Gogh.

But the circle of Les XX was not simply a group of artists who wished to exhibit together, it was also a state of mind, a willingness to welcome novelty in all fields – artistic, literary and musical. 'Right across the board, the battle against routine was engaged', Octave Maus would say. From the time of their first exhibition, a programme of concerts and lectures was held. The interest of the *vingtistes* in music was soon increased tenfold by the presence in Brussels of Vincent d'Indy and Eugène Ysaïe, who introduced modern French music – by Saint-Saëns, Chabrier and Chausson – to the public at large.

But after ten years of existence, Les XX was dissolved to put an end to the internal dissension and conflicts that hindered the successful organization of the salons. The changing of the guard was accomplished with the creation of La Libre Esthétique (1894-1914), which had Octave Maus as it only director and 'inviter', while the organizing committee was formed of one hundred members chosen from supportive intellectuals (critics, collectors, even businessmen) but included no artists. Maus formulated the exhibitions on the basis of avant-garde movements discovered by Les XX. Thus the works of impressionists, neo-impressionists and symbolists continued to be presented, and the section devoted to the decorative arts was considerably enlarged. These salons largely contributed to the spread of different forms of thought that developed in the late nineteenth century and persisted well into the twentieth century.

THÉO VAN RYSSELBERGHE, Portrait of Émile Verhaeren, *1915*
Oil on canvas, 80 × 100 cm
Inv. 4111

This portrait was made of Verhaeren the year before his accidental death in 1916. A contributor since the start of his career to the reviews *La Jeune Belgique* and *L'Art moderne*, Verhaeren was won over to the symbolist movement after being a member of the Parnassian group. His poetry of 'paroxysm' is also a poetry of 'suggestion' in which the reader is asked to realize, through his own feelings, the poet's vision, which is like a 'whistle in the darkness'. A shrewd art critic, Verhaeren was notable for his championing of Vogels and Ensor.

FERNAND KHNOPFF, Portrait of Edmond Picard, *1884*
Oil on canvas, 40.5 × 32.5 cm
Inv. 12204

A socialist and a champion of universal suffrage, the jurist Edmond Picard (1836-1924) was also a passionate enthusiast of literature and art. He was one of the founders of the review *L'Art moderne*, in which he advocated 'social art' rather than the notion of art for art's sake upheld by *La Jeune Belgique*. An occasional patron of the arts, he supported Auguste Rodin, even organizing an exhibition of the sculptor's work in his town house in 1899.

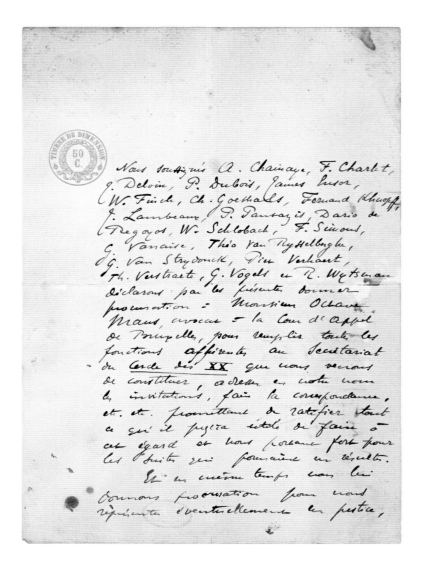
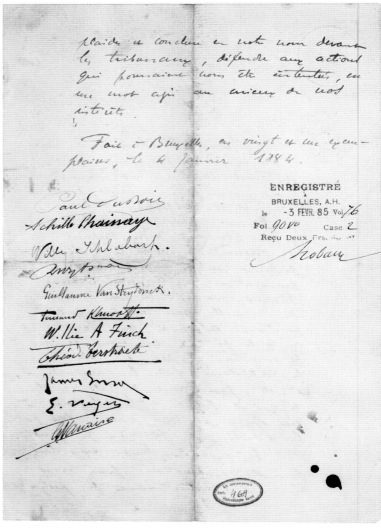

Charter of the group Les XX, appointing Octave Maus as secretary,
Brussels, 4 January 1884, 25.2 × 17.8 cm
Inv. AACB 4609

View of the room of the first
Salon des XX, with works by
John Singer Sargent, James Ensor,
Fernand Khnopff, Jef Lambeaux,
Auguste Rodin and Paul Devigne,
Palais des Beaux-Arts, Brussels,
2 February–2 March1884,
18 × 23.7 cm
Inv. AACB 4653

Poster for the first Salon des XX,
Palais des Beaux-Arts, Brussels,
2 February–2 March 1884,
87.9 × 60.1 cm
Inv. AACB 11.357

PALAIS DES BEAUX-ARTS

FÉVRIER 1884

LES XX BRUXELLES

EXPOSITION

INTERNATIONALE

de PEINTURE & de SCULPTURE

Organisée par les XX

Artistes invités

Belgique. Artan, Heymans, Rops, Stobbaerts, De Vigne, Van der Stappen, Vinçotte.

France. Gervex, Roty, Injalbert, Rodin.

Hollande. Israëls, Maris, Mauve.

Angleterre. Stott, Whistler.

Allemagne. Liebermann.

Suède-Norwège. Bergh.

Etats-Unis. Chase, Sargent.

Vingtistes

A. Chainaye
F. Charlet
J. Delvin
P. Dubois
J. Ensor
W. Finch
Ch. Goethals
F. Khnopff
J. Lambeaux
P. Pantazis
D. de Regoyos
W. Schlobach
F. Simons
G. Vanaise
Th. Van Rysselberghe
G. Van Strydonck
P. Verhaert
Th. Verstraete
G. Vogels
R. Wytsman

Ouverture Samedi 2 Février, à 2 heures

A partir du lendemain, l'exposition sera ouverte au public, tous les jours, de 10 à 5 heures, du 3 Février au 1er Mars

PRIX D'ENTRÉE : Le Samedi . . . . 2 FRANCS.
Les autres jours . . . . 50 CENTIMES.

Le Trésorier, VICTOR BERNIER.

Le Secrétaire, OCTAVE MAUS.

Bruxelles. — Imprimerie et Lithographie E. LAMBERT-STEVELINCK, rue de la Pacification, 31

Postcard from Théo van Rysselberghe to Octave Maus with the design for the poster for the sixth Salon du Cercle La Libre Esthétique, Brussels, 24 January 1897, 14.2 × 9.1 cm
Inv. AACB 6333

Programme of the third concert of modern works given during the ninth Salon des XX in Brussels, 4 March 1892, 21.3 × 13.7 cm
Inv. AACB 79.642

Poster for the fourth Salon du Cercle
La Libre Esthétique, designed by
Gisbert Combaz, Brussels, Musée
Moderne, 25 February–1 April 1897,
73.3 × 43.8 cm
Inv. AACB 118.592

VAN NU EN STRAKS

The example of the French-language review *La Jeune Belgique* and the growing influence of the militant Netherlandish periodical *De Nieuwe Gids* encouraged Dutch speakers to create their own review in 1893, *Van Nu en Straks*, at the initiative of August Vermeylen. 'Devoted to the art of today, curious about the art of the future here and abroad', the publication was to run for twenty-five issues (the last in 1901). It was noteworthy for the quality of its paper, its typography and its large format, as well as for the illustrations to which James Ensor, Georges Lemmen, George Morren, Henry van de Velde, Théo van Rysselberghe, Jan Toorop and others contributed. Initially inspired by French symbolism and stoked by socialist and even anarchist thought, it would later appoint itself the defender of the fin-de-siècle idealist movement and help pave the way for the development of art nouveau in Dutch-speaking Belgium.

Cover of the review Van Nu en Straks, *no. 2, 1893. Initial letter by Henry van de Velde*
Bibliothèque Royale de Belgique, Brussels. Inv. FSX1045A

NEO-IMPRESSIONISM

"Although Belgian artists gathered at the sides of the neo-impressionists, it was not simply out of fascination for the modernity of Paris, but also through a desire to take positivist thinking to the limit."

In May 1886 an exhibition of the impressionists was held in Paris – the eighth and last by the group founded in 1874 – of which the most striking episode was the presentation of the large manifesto work by Georges Seurat, *A Sunday on La Grande Jatte*, painted, as is well known, using the pointillist or divisionist technique. Novelty, scandal, mockery: there was plenty to arouse the curiosity of Émile Verhaeren, who was then in Paris, and he alerted Théo van Rysselberghe and Octave Maus. Completely won over, Maus described Seurat as the "Messiah of a new art" and did not hesitate to convince Les XX to invite the artist, along with Pissarro and Signac, to the exhibition the following year that would be titled *The Parisian Vingtistes*.

The exhibition of the pointillists was held in Brussels in 1887 to great public success, as Signac wrote to Pissarro: "I left the exhibition of the XX exhausted. An enormous crowd, a dreadful crush, very typically bourgeois with their anti-art attitude. In short, a very great success for us: Seurat's canvas was invisible, impossible to get close the crowd was so large." But curiosity was not sufficient for Maus, so, wishing to explain the key points of pointillist art to the public, *L'Art moderne* published a series of articles to draw attention to the historic importance of neo-impressionism. One of the most convincing contributions was by Félix Fénéon, the review's French correspondent, who took advantage of the platform to publish the first theoretical exposé of

the new technique. He confirmed that impressionism was by then outmoded, to the benefit of a mode of painting whose technique had been developed from scientific principles borrowed from the studies of Michel-Eugène Chevreul: the decomposition of light into the colours of the prism, and the optical mix created when the eye blends juxtaposed touches of pure colour. The goal of the new art was not to capture the fleeting instant, said Fénéon, but to "synthesize the landscape in its definitive aspect".

Belgian artists were very attentive to these arguments, which were redefining modernity, but Stevens and Khnopff were unconvinced. Others would see divisionism as idealistic, for example, Henry van de Velde, whose articles, unlike Fénéon's insistence on the technique's scientific foundation, offered a symbolist interpretation of Seurat's work, claiming that the aim of neo-impressionism lay "beyond reality". Encouraged by Paul Signac, the first Belgian painter to try the technique was Willy Finch during the winter of 1887–88, then others rallied to this new "school of the stipple". However, some developed their personal touch, such as Théo van Rysselberghe and Georges Lemmen, who won renown as portraitists, and Anna Boch, Henry van de Velde and the Dutchman Jan Toorop, who had settled in Brussels and joined Les XX.

Raised in a middle-class milieu in Ghent, Théo van Rysselberghe had studied at the Académie de Bruxelles in the studio of Jean-François Portaels, an orientalist painter and talented portraitist who found his pupil a worthy heir. Curious by nature, van Rysselberghe travelled and, like his master, visited North Africa where he produced some outstanding paintings (see p. 87). A founding member of Les XX in 1883, van Rysselberghe became the friend and

GEORGES SEURAT, **The Seine at La Grande Jatte,** *1888*
Oil on canvas, 65 × 82 cm
Inv. 5091

A small island on the edge of Paris, La Grande Jatte was a popular Sunday destination, where visitors would walk, dance and practise water sports. It enjoyed international renown following Seurat's painting *A Sunday on La Grande Jatte*, the manifesto of neo-impressionism. The canvas exhibited here, also painted using the scientific colour theory, was first owned by the painter and collector Anna Boch, who bequeathed it to the Musée des Beaux-Arts in Brussels.

PAUL SIGNAC, **The Calanque (The Bay),** *1906*
Oil on canvas, 73 × 93 cm
Inv. 5090

A follower of divisionism right from the start, Paul Signac
(1863-1935) never completely discarded it, though he gave
up pure pointillism in favour of a broader touch. The shore
at Saint-Tropez, where he moved in 1892, was a source
of recurrent inspiration for him. It also provided motifs
to Théo van Rysselberghe, who became a close friend
of Signac's, with whom he shared a passion for sailing.

VINCENT VAN GOGH, **Seascape at Saintes-Maries-de-la-Mer,** *1888*
Crayon and ink on paper, 24.2 × 31.6 cm
Inv. 6743

While living in Arles in Provence, Vincent van Gogh
(1853–1890) visited Saintes-Maries-de-la-Mer in May 1888,
which inspired him to produce a dozen works. This ink
drawing made with a reed pen is one of three versions (the
only one to be signed) of the same seascape. Taking the
Japanese style of drawing that he was fascinated by as his
starting point, van Gogh succeeds in suggesting with a single
line the dazzle of the light and the changing colours of the
sea. Exhibited at Les XX in 1891, this drawing was given to
Octave Maus by its owner, Johanna van Gogh–Bonger, the
artist's sister-in-law. As the ink is damaged by the light, this
fragile sheet requires very special conditions of conservation
and can only be displayed on very rare occasions.

AUGUSTE RODIN,
**Fallen Caryatid Carrying
Her Stone,** *1881–97 (?)
Seated statue, stone,
62.5 × 46 × 43.5 cm
Inv. 3516*

advisor of Octave Maus. He was a fervent admirer of Whistler, Degas and Toulouse-Lautrec, but the real shock came when, at the age of twenty-four, he discovered the art of Seurat. Fascinated by the chromo-luminarist revolution, he gave himself over completely to the divisionist technique that satisfied both his fondness for precision and his aspirations as a colourist. His remarkable talent as a portraitist allowed him to produce works of great psychological depth (*Portrait of Octave Maus*, p. 56). When, later, he found pointillism too restrictive, he used broader, freer touches (*The Promenade*, 1901), thus demonstrating that he was not a 'follower' and that he was not losing any of his inventiveness.

Although Belgian artists gathered at the sides of the neo-impressionists, it was not simply out of fascination for the modernity of Paris, but also through a desire to take positivist thinking to the limit, as scientific progress was thought to be an instrument for social emancipation. In the wake of Signac's anarchist commitment, Henry van de Velde wished to give a modern form to his social aspirations and so took up divisionism in 1888, employing it in his series of paintings of life in the countryside

(*Faits du village*, 1890) and his architecturally constructed landscapes in which he began his theoretical deliberation on the use of the line, which was to lead him to 'invent' art nouveau. No longer content to be a painter, he worked also as an architect, a decorator and a craftsman, beginning with the construction of his own house, Bloemenwerf, in 1895.

As importers of neo-impressionism, the circle of Les XX also invited other great French artists to Belgium, such as Rodin, whose attachment to the country was longstanding. He had visited Belgium several times since 1870 in search of work and sculpted, among others, the caryatids on the Brussels Stock Exchange. It was in the capital that he also had the idea for his first masterpiece, *The Age of Bronze*. It was at first contested that this work had been cast from a mould, but was awarded a gold medal in Ghent in 1880. Invited to the first Vingtiste salon in 1884, Rodin was elected a member of the group four years later, allowing him to exhibit each year. Championed in particular by Edmond Picard, co-director of *L'Art moderne*, and Émile Verhaeren, Rodin discovered an enthusiastic and faithful public in Belgium that greatly contributed to his fame.

AUGUSTE RODIN, One of the Burghers of Calais:
Jean d'Aire, *1886–90*
Statue, bronze, 204.5 × 71.5 × 66.5 cm
Inv. 4905

THÉO VAN RYSSELBERGHE, **The Promenade**, *1901*
Oil on canvas, 97 × 130 cm
Inv. 3745

Both a landscape and a group portrait, this painting
shows a moment during a holiday in Ambleteuse,
a coastal resort in the Pas-de-Calais, where
van Rysselberghe (1862–1926) and his wife Maria
frequently stayed at the invitation of musician
Georges Flé. The composition is especially
remarkable, with four vertical female figures
standing out against the horizontality of the sea.
The graceful group are tinged with tones of pink,
blue and white, characteristic of the artist's palette
during those years.

WILLY FINCH, Coastal Landscape, c. *1892*
Oil on canvas, 35 × 55 cm
Inv. 12.196

HENRY VAN DE VELDE, Faits du village. VII.
Girl Darning a Stocking, *1890*
Oil on canvas, 78 × 101.5 cm
Inv. 7797

This painting is from Henry van de Velde's brief pointillist
period, which lasted from 1888 to 1890 and encompassed
no more than twelve works. The series of canvases titled
Faits du village, of which this is the seventh, was painted
in Campine, near Antwerp, where the artist lived
from 1886 to 1890. In this work he has perfected
his pointillist research while adding his own conception of
the painting. His technical skill and compositional sense
are united, not without lyricism, to suggest the
harmony of nature and the peace of village life.

THÉO VAN RYSSELBERGHE,
Portrait of Mrs Charles Maus, *1890*
Oil on canvas, 56 × 47 cm
Inv. 6384

POST-IMPRESSIONISTS AND NABIS

"Remember that a painting, before being a battle horse, a nude woman or some anecdote, is essentially a flat surface covered with colours assembled in a certain order."

Paul Gauguin was represented for the first time at the exhibitions of Les XX in February 1889, when he presented twelve paintings executed in Brittany. This was the same year that he organized the famous exhibition of the "impressionist and synthetist group" at the Café Volpini, which constituted a manifesto of the theories he had recently developed with Émile Bernard. He abandoned impressionism, which he considered an expression of realism, in order to focus his attention on line, colour and form, in an approach he termed synthetism. The synthesis was primarily plastic, as Maurice Denis explained the following year with his famous formula: "Remember that a painting, before being a battle horse, a nude woman or some anecdote, is essentially a flat surface covered with colours assembled in a certain order." Gauguin's goal was to attain a "modern style" by simplifying the means and reducing the image to forms of pure colour which he assembled for rigorously decorative purposes, and from which perspective and depth were proscribed. In addition to the pictorial technique entailed – the use of flat tints – synthetism was a means for the artist to express an idea or a feeling without concerning himself with objective reality. "Art is above all a means of expression, a creation of our spirit, for which nature is simply a vehicle", as would later be written by Maurice Denis, the "Nabi with beautiful icons". It is easy to understand, therefore, why in Belgium Gauguin was rapidly considered a major representative of pictorial symbolism.

Gauguin's name reappeared at the 1891 exhibition of Les XX but it was not until 1894 that he visited Brussels in person. Invited by Octave Maus to exhibit at the first Salon de La Libre Esthétique, he presented paintings he had brought back from Tahiti. The list of guest artists that year included the names of Maurice Denis, Paul Ranson and Henri-Gabriel Ibels, some of the founding members of the Nabi group. There is nothing surprising about their presence at the show as these young artists had also broken with academicism. As admirers of Gauguin, they wished to rediscover the "sacred" nature of painting and instil art with a new spirituality – after all, the word "nabi" is Hebrew for prophet – an aspiration that harmonized totally with the aims of symbolism. The influence of synthetism, combined with their love of Japanese art, prompted these artists to question the value of traditional perspective and concentrate on the ornamental character of line and form, elements that were to become the essence of art nouveau. Another link with the art circles of Belgium was the Nabis' interest in craftsmanship and the applied arts because, like Gauguin, they wanted to do away with the old-fashioned concept of major and minor arts, and to abandon easel painting in order to associate painting, sculpture and engraving with the decorative arts and thus create a synthesis of all the arts.

The Antwerp-based circle L'Association pour l'Art was the first to give the Nabis the opportunity to

PAUL GAUGUIN, **The Breton Calvary**, or **The Green Christ**, *1889*
Oil on canvas, 92 × 73.5 cm
Inv. 4416

With its solid, simplified forms, vigorous contours, and strong, unreal colours, this painting may be considered the acme of Gauguin's synthetism. The artist uses the image of the Breton countrywoman, who seems to be absorbed by the stone pietà behind her, to correlate daily life and religious life, the temporal and the spiritual. In accordance with the symbolist spirit, the painting is not a window looking out onto the world but a subjective reproduction of a personal experience.

exhibit the full range of their activities. In 1892, invited by Max Elskamp and Henry van de Velde, Pierre Bonnard was the only Nabi, but the following year Ranson, Denis, Ibels, Bonnard and Vuillard were present with paintings, decorative projects, fans and lithographs. In 1895 some of them sent works to the exhibition of applied arts in Liège. The production of the Nabis, which was presented in this manner each year in Belgium, was consistent with that of Belgian artists of identical aspirations.

The attention paid by the Nabis in their paintings to daily life, street scenes and childhood, which they treated with humour and feeling, is also seen in the works of Belgian painter Henri Evenepoel; in spite of a career cut short by typhoid at the age of twenty-seven, he left an oeuvre of rare quality, a veritable synthesis of the modernist currents in the late nineteenth century. After receiving training at the Académie de Bruxelles, in 1892 he left for Paris to attend courses in decorative art at the École des Beaux-Arts, but he quickly gave them up to study in the atelier of Gustave Moreau alongside pupils Matisse and Rouault. He very soon learned to take pleasure in sketching Parisian life and the bustle in the streets and cafés. This led to his 1896 painting *The Cellar at the Soleil d'Or*, an atmospheric scene whose perspicacity owes much to his admiration for Toulouse-Lautrec. He shortly developed his favourite genre, portraiture, in which he was able to employ his psychological insight and talent as an observer. He was above all inspired by childhood, for which he used as models the children of his cousin Louise, with whom he was united in love and by whom he had a son, and it was with great awareness and understanding that he portrayed their innocence and poetry (*Henriette in a Large Hat*, 1899). He used different scenes from daily life as motifs to create paintings that astonish with the synthesis of the forms, and the use of contiguous tones and values that bring the ensemble of planes forward to the surface of the canvas. And in doing so he coincided with the preoccupations of the Nabis, Vuillard and Vallotton in particular, whose works Evenepoel had seen at the Indépendants. Sent to Algeria in the winter of 1897–98 on account of his precarious health, but also to separate him from Louise, he was confronted by intense light that was difficult to render on canvas without detriment to the forms. *The Orange Market in Blidah*, constituted by large flat tints, demonstrates that he had brilliantly passed from an impressionist touch to a synthetist conception of his art.

ÉDOUARD VUILLARD, **Two Schoolchildren**, *1894*
Distemper on canvas, 214 × 98 cm
Inv. 6681

This painting was one of nine that composed the series *Gardens*, today dispersed. It was painted to decorate the home of Alexandre Natanson, one of the three founders of the famous Paris magazine *La Revue blanche*, who was a friend to all the members of the avant-garde during the 1890s. The emphasis on verticality of its format was directly inspired by the Japanese art so admired by the Nabis, of whom Vuillard (1868–1940) was a member. The decorative nature of this work harmonizes with the aesthetic embraced by the group, which had given itself the objective of removing the distinctions between the arts.

PIERRE BONNARD, Nude Against the Light, c. 1908
Oil on canvas, 124.5 × 109 cm
Inv. 6519

Around 1900, the Nabi group had split up and, although they maintained their friendship, its members had embarked on their individual paths. Pierre Bonnard (1867–1947) tackled a new theme, the nude, using his companion Marthe as his only model. Renouncing the flat tints of his youthful works, he rediscovered modelling, perspective and depth by introducing, as is seen here, the unobtrusive interplay of mirrors and reflections. He lightened his palette, let air circulate around the body and the objects, and recuperated the light characteristic of impressionism. This painting was exhibited in 1909 at La Libre Esthétique, where it was purchased by Octave Maus.

HENRI EVENEPOEL, **The Cellar at the Soleil d'Or,** *1896*
Oil on canvas, 73.5 × 92 cm
Inv. 7668

Scenes from contemporary life, one of the favourite
themes of the impressionists, inspired Evenepoel
(1872-1899) to paint this interior of a Parisian café.
Against a background rendered in muted tones, the
atmospheric painting sets figures portrayed with a
perceptiveness typical of Toulouse-Lautrec; their
comical, true-to-life postures are also characteristic
of this master admired by the Belgian artist.

∨ HENRI EVENEPOEL, **The Orange Market in Blidah,** *1898*
∨ *Oil on canvas, 81 × 125 cm*
Inv. 6171

Fired by the avant-garde art of Paris, in particular
the modernity of the Nabis, Evenepoel (1872-1899)
gradually moved away from the impressionist
technique. The powerful light of North Africa led
him to adopt warm colours and a reduced chromatic
range. Simplification of the contours and layout,
and the use of flat tints were all characteristics
that heralded fauvism.

HENRI EVENEPOEL, Man in Red / Portrait of the Painter
Paul Baignères, *1894*
Oil on canvas, 225 × 151 cm
Inv. 3753

∨   *Self-portrait in a mirror, photograph taken by
Henri Evenepoel in his studio in the Avenue
de la Motte-Picquet, Paris, October 1897*
Inv. AACB 76.613/115

∨   *Charles and Henriette de Mey walking in the
Place de la Concorde, Paris. Photograph taken
by Henri Evenepoel, autumn 1898*
Inv. AACB 76.613/28

HENRI EVENEPOEL,
Henriette in a Large Hat, *1899*
Oil on canvas, 72 × 58 cm
Inv. 4939

BELGIAN IMPRESSIONISM

"How was it possible to disavow the influence of France at a time when exchanges were increasing, and Belgian artists made frequent visits to Paris, discovered a lighter palette and thus nurtured their own thinking?"

The question of whether there was a specifically 'Belgian impressionism' was the subject of lively debate among art critics as from 1880, when the *Exposition historique de l'Art belge* reviewed fifty years of the country's art. For, although the term 'impressionism' alluded to French painters, their practice of painting outdoors to capture the effects of the light and atmosphere was not their prerogative, as some realists, such as Louis Artan, had similarly adopted it during the 1870s. But how was it possible to disavow the influence of France at a time when exchanges were increasing, and Belgian artists made frequent visits to Paris, discovered a lighter palette and thus nurtured their own thinking? Opinions were divided between the upholders of a Belgian impressionism that had deeply national roots, the position held by Camille Lemonnier, and others, notably in *L'Art moderne*, who considered the oeuvre of certain painters to be derived from that of French artists. In the twentieth century, art historians tackled the question once again, and identified two currents of Belgian impressionism: one imported and more intellectual in character that would lead to pointillism, and a more visceral, home-grown impressionism that developed into expressionism. But that is no more than the sketchiest outline of a situation in constant development: the fin-de-siècle art of Belgium was marked by perpetual evolution and a wide range of outside influences that were exerted as much through the glorious Flemish art of the past as by contemporary foreign sources.

'The most difficult thing is not to paint a landscape but to create the luminous impression of that landscape', said Guillaume Vogels. Although his words are very similar to the aims of French impressionism – this artist has sometimes been considered an epigone of the movement – Vogels' art is much more rooted in the national realist tradition. Following an early period characterized by a certain romanticism, he turned his attention to naturalism under the influence of Hippolyte Boulenger and Louis Artan, with whom he painted direct from the motif in 1873 in Anseremme. His art then experienced spectacular development: he abandoned the naturalist aesthetic

Guillaume Vogels, Mist, *undated*
Watercolour and gouache on paper,
25.2 × 17.2 cm
Inv. 6565

GUILLAUME VOGELS,
Snow, Evening, c. 1883
Oil on canvas, 105 × 154 cm
Inv. 3770

This painting succeeds magnificently in blending a realist depiction of the landscape with impressionist subjectivity. The transient moment captured here is when the sun has just disappeared but continues to set the sky ablaze, here tingeing the fluffy snow with pinkish highlights. The coarse application of the paint with brush and palette knife is typical of Vogels' manner from the 1880s on.

and adopted much greater freedom in his execution, working the matter with a palette knife and introducing innovations into the organization of the forms, colours and pictorial space. However, the modernity of his manner would long remain beyond the comprehension of the public and critics. He participated in three of the four Chrysalide exhibitions, in 1877, 1878 and 1881. Also present at the last of these was James Ensor, on whom Vogel's influence would be decisive. Two years later, in 1883, Vogel became a founding member of Les XX where he enjoyed support among its milieu. At the first Salon des XX, Émile Verhaeren declared, "Vogels is a master. He is gifted in every field. . . . He has both a manner and a mark." However, Vogels also had his detractors owing to the "sketchy" nature of his works and his use of thick impasto. It was only very late that recognition was given to Vogels' originality, his capacity to infuse the pictorial space with new dynamism, and to liberate the relationship between form and light from all stylistic convention inherited from the past. It then became possible to identify him as a precursor of Flemish expressionism.

Contrary to Vogels, who was completely anchored in his homeland, Émile Claus is the perfect example of a painter who was influenced by the French artists without relinquishing his own character. Whereas his early works were marked by sentimental and narrative realism, they rapidly developed as a result of his friendship with Camille Lemonnier. Lemonnier encouraged him to turn away from academic constraints, to leave the studio and go out into nature, and to user lighter colours. Settled on the banks of the River Lys, Claus became a painter of country life and the light in the manner of French painter Jules Bastien-Lepage, of whom he was a great admirer. A stay in Paris between 1889 and 1892 allowed him to discover the impressionists, in particular Pissarro, Monet and Renoir. He took their examples to heart and, gradually, figures faded out of his landscapes to make way for investigations into the rendering of atmosphere and light. A founder member of the circle Vie et Lumière in 1904, of which Ensor and Lemmen in particular were members, Claus organized exhibitions to which he issued invitations to foreign painters who shared his "luminist" vision of painting. A great traveller, Claus visited Spain, Algeria and Morocco, and twice visited Venice, whose distinctive light fascinated him. His views of the Grand Canal heralded those he was to paint in London during his exile in Great Britain between 1914 and 1919. In these works Claus unstintingly painted the Thames and its bridges from above, altering his rapid touch and palette to suit the changing light of the hour of the day and the season.

The only woman to have been a member of Les XX, Anna Boch, born into a wealthy family, had the painter Eugène Boch as her brother, and Octave Maus as a cousin, who introduced her into intellectual circles. Having received a conventional artistic education, a new direction was opened up to her when she discovered plein-air painters like Boulenger and Baron. The teachings of the landscape painter Isadore Verheyden, an enthusiastic painter of nature, led her to lighten her palette and refine her style. She made her artistic debut at the 1884 Brussels Triennial, and two years later joined Les XX, subsequently taking part in all their exhibitions. Her acquaintance with Théo van Rysselberghe, who introduced her to the neo-impressionist technique, resulted in her execution of several pointillist paintings. The doubt she felt at its systemic nature encouraged her to gradually move away from the technique to adopt a broader, freer touch. Around the turn of the century, she travelled a great deal, in particular in France, Holland, Italy, Germany, Greece and Morocco, where she painted landscapes and seascapes. Later, through association with the fauve trend, her painting became more constructed and her handling of the paint freer. A knowledgeable and bold collector, she acquired works by her contemporaries, notably a van Gogh, *The Red Vineyard*, the only painting to have been sold during the artist's lifetime; thus, Anna Boch also contributed to the cultural life of the capital in her role as art patron. In addition to the gifts she made during her life (Ensor's *Russian Music*, p. 46), the bequest she left to the Musées royaux des Beaux-Arts de Belgique enriched its collections with such outstanding works as *Conversation in the Pasture: Pont-Aven* by Gauguin, *The Seine at the Grande Jatte* by Seurat, and *La Calanque (The Bay)* by Signac.

THÉO VAN RYSSELBERGHE, **Arabian Fantasia,** *1884*
Oil on canvas, 170 × 300 cm
Inv. 4139

Before becoming a fervent adept of neo-impressionism, van Rysselberghe
(1862–1926) began his career as a painter with the production of dark
works in the romantic or realist tradition. His first exhibition, in Ghent in
1881, won him a municipal grant, which he used to visit Spain and Morocco
in the company of Constantin Meunier. He returned from a second trip
to Morocco, in 1883–84, with this large *Arabian Fantasia.* Impressed by
the African light, van Rysselberghe lightened his palette, a development
that led him to adopt pointillism a few years later.

ÉMILE CLAUS, **Cows Crossing the River Lys,** *1899*   >>
Oil on canvas, 200 × 305 cm
Inv. 3584

ANNA BOCH, **Coast of Brittany**, c. *1901*
Oil on canvas, 108 × 146.5 cm
Inv. 3625

This seascape, painted during a trip Anna Boch (1848–1936)
made to Brittany, blends characteristics of realist painting
with the light touches typical of impressionism. The harshness
of the cliffs creates a splendid contrast with the brilliant and
light treatment of the sky and water. Solidity and finesse are
representative traits of this painter, who won wide admiration
from her colleagues.

ÉMILE CLAUS, **Harvesting Flax**, *1904*
Oil on canvas, 156.5 × 201 cm
Inv. 3769

ÉMILE CLAUS, View of London: Waterloo Bridge, Sun and Rain,
March 1916
Oil on canvas, 102 × 127 cm
Inv. 4298

This painting ineluctably calls to mind the series of London
views painted by Monet between 1903 and 1905. More than
ten years later, Claus (1849–1924), a great admirer of the
French master, tackled identical motifs with equally remarkable
atmospheric effects. This work is a sort of acme of 'luminism',
a term given to the oeuvre of Belgian painters who attempted
to capture light and fleeting impressions.

Total art
New
expressions

ART NOUVEAU ARCHITECTURE

"The decorative elements inspired by plants were created, as Horta recommended, by 'throwing away the flower and keeping the stem', and in complete harmony with the interior spaces, where sinuous arabesques rose unbroken from floor to ceiling, and even embraced the furniture."

The outpouring of decorative arts initiated by modernist and social ambitions in Belgium in the late nineteenth century found its ultimate manifestation in architecture, which consequently underwent a far-reaching transformation of the understanding of space and the conception of interior decoration. Three names dominated in what would become Belgian art nouveau architecture, those of Victor Horta, Paul Hankar and Henry van de Velde, who would be both its theoreticians and its initiators.

Born in Ghent in 1861, Victor Horta was sent to Paris by his parents to study interior decoration. During his stay there he became interested in new materials like steel and industrial glass, and also discovered the theories of Eugène Viollet-le-Duc in *Entretiens sur l'architecture* (1863 and 1872). On his return to Belgium, Horta became such a brilliant student at the Académie des Beaux-Arts that he was employed by Alphonse Balat, the architect to the king, with whom he designed the royal greenhouses of Laeken. From Balat, Horta learned to ensure every detail was perfect but he rejected the notion of referring to the

past exclusively for inspiration. In 1885 Horta began to construct small buildings and develop his own vision, which led him to prefer curves to straight lines in the belief that they increase the impression of space and offer better support in construction. His ideas became increasingly defined as his apprenticeship progressed, for example, he took issue at the different manner with which architecture and construction were viewed and refuted the belief that only an engineer was authorized to introduce innovation. He was one of the first to understand the ornamental potential of iron and to consider glass a fundamental feature of architecture. His professional career began properly in 1893 when he was commissioned to design two houses: those of Émile Tassel, a professor of geometry at the Université de Bruxelles, and Eugène Autrique, a famous lawyer, who introduced Horta into the sophisticated circles of Brussels where he would find many of his clients. These were followed by commission to design the town house of Armand Solvay, a project that marked the real arrival of art nouveau in architecture. The design contained everything that would come to define Horta's architecture: curved blocks of stone on the facade, a strongly evident metal structure, asymmetry, glass doors, and the free circulation of air and light. The decorative elements inspired by plants were created, as Horta recommended, by 'throwing away the flower and keeping the stem', and in complete harmony with the interior spaces, where sinuous arabesques rose unbroken from floor to ceiling, and even embraced the furniture, also designed by Horta. The architect's goal of creating a 'total work of art' was thus achieved. Horta's vision was further diffused with construction of the townhouse of Octave Aubecq (1899–1903, destroyed), the design of its outstanding set of furniture, today sadly dispersed, and with the building of his own house-cum-studio in 1898. One of his most famous designs was for the Maison du Peuple (1895–99, destroyed in 1965), commissioned by the Belgian Workers' Party. This he had conceived as 'a palace

VICTOR HORTA, *Main hall and staircase of the Aubecq residence, 1899–1903, demolished, Avenue Louise, Brussels Musée Horta, Saint-Gilles (Brussels), Fondation Jean et Renée Delhaye*

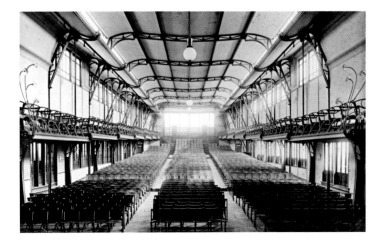

VICTOR HORTA, *The entertainment room in the Maison du Peuple, 1895–99, demolished, Rue Joseph-Stevens, Brussels Musée Horta, Saint-Gilles (Brussels), Fondation Jean et Renée Delhaye*

BRUXELLES. — La Maison du Peuple

VICTOR HORTA,
*Maison du Peuple,
1895–99, demolished, Rue
Joseph-Stevens, Brussels
Musée Horta, Saint-Gilles
(Brussels), Fondation Jean
et Renée Delhaye*

that would not be a palace but a 'house', where the air and light would be the luxury so long proscribed from workers' slums'. Shortly afterwards, Horta began to receive a flow of public commissions: in Tournai the Musée des Beaux-Arts, and in Brussels the Centre Hospitalier Universitaire Brugmann, the Palais des Beaux-Arts and the Gare Centrale, though he died before this last project was completed.

However, art nouveau was not the exclusive preserve of Victor Horta: he had a competitor in the very active Paul Hankar, his former fellow student, whose practice was shaped by his theoretical consideration of the arts and his commitment to social architecture. Although Hankar also favoured asymmetry and curves, he differed in his taste for polychromy and the different manner with which the materials were treated. He received valuable assistance from his partner, Adolphe Crespin, an early lover of Japanese art, who was very fond of studying nature and suggested decorations that played a major role in the stylization developed by art nouveau architects. One of Paul Hankar's masterpieces is the house of the symbolist Albert Ciamberlani in Ixelles, in which the facade is decorated using sgraffito to allow the metal structure beneath to appear. The building is a perfect application of the rationalist theories of Viollet-le-Duc, who argued that the ornamentation of a building should be linked to its structure, and that the design of the facade should follow from the organization of the internal spaces. In addition to private houses, Hankar designed several shops, in which his attention was not focused purely on the front but extended to every last detail of the furnishings and decoration inside. Unfortunately, not a single one has survived.

JOSEF HOFFMANN, *Stoclet House, 1905–11, Avenue de Tervueren, Woluwe-Saint-Pierre (Brussels)*

STOCLET HOUSE

Built between 1905 and 1911 at 279 avenue de Tervueren in Brussels, Stoclet House was designed by the Austrian architect Josef Hoffmann, a member of the Viennese Secession, for the director of the Société Générale Adolphe Stoclet. Breaking entirely with the art nouveau aesthetic, the austere facade clad with white marble is formed by geometric volumes whose edges are emphasized by thick bronze beading. Its gleaming surfaces are unbroken and uniformly flat. The interior is a perfect synthesis of styles in which a wide variety of techniques and materials have been used: the friezes in the dining room – *L'Attente* and *L'Accomplissement* – designed by Gustav Klimt have affinities with Byzantine mosaics. Crowned by four sculptures by Franz Metzner, the tower accommodates a staircase and private and service spaces. The workshops of the Wiener Werkstätte, founded in Vienna by Josef Hoffmann, Kolomann Moser and Fritz Waerndorfer, produced all the elements used in the interior decoration, including the furniture, central lights, crockery and silverware. This residence is the only surviving *Gesamtkunstwerk* (total work of art) elaborated by the Wiener Werkstätte.

HENRY VAN DE VELDE'S *private residence, Bloemenwerf, 1895, Avenue Vanderaey, Uccle (Brussels) Archives d'Architecture Moderne, Brussels*

After giving up painting and long arguing that the distinction between the major and minor arts should be abolished, Henry van de Velde made his convictions public in 1894 in an essay titled *Déblaiement d'art*, in which he argued for a new art ('art nouveau') founded on morality and the union of the arts. He also placed insistence on use of the line, which is both a carrier and the result of an emotion, as well as a force that derives its vitality from the person who draws it: in short, it is an embodiment of life. Application of his theories followed soon after and in 1895, without any architectural training, he designed his own house (Bloemenwerf, or Court of Flowers) in Uccle. The yel-

low bricks, small-squared windows, three gables with wooden laths, and the porch over the front steps are features similar to those of English cottages published in the review *The Studio*. The layout of the rooms was also inspired by Arts and Crafts architecture, while the furniture, also designed by van de Velde, reveals his preoccupation with lines. It was his belief that a space derives its energy from the dynamism of its lines. The garden was also English in style and designed by Maria Sèthe, the artist's wife. In the years that followed, van de Velde's architectural work was restricted to the interior decoration of the houses of Paul Otlet and Florence de Brouckère. His design in Paris for the interior of Samuel Bing's shop L'Art Nouveau aroused little interest and finally it was from Germany that his major commissions came. Thus, in 1900, the family upped sticks for Berlin, where van de Velde set up his new studio.

Initiated by these three important individuals, art nouveau architecture was continued by lesser talents who concerned themselves only with a building's appearance, without linking this to its structural logic. Treated industrially by construction companies so that occasionally entire streets of buildings would have art nouveau facades, the aesthetic eventually wearied the progressive bourgeoisie, who spurned it in favour of geometric forms. With interest in it waning, the splendid heritage represented by art nouveau architecture was increasingly demolished.

ÉDOUARD PELSENEER *and* FERNAND KHNOPFF, *House-cum-studio of Fernand Khnopff, 1900, demolished, Avenue des Courses, Ixelles (Brussels) Archives d'Architecture Moderne, Brussels*

PAUL SAINTENOY, *art nouveau annexe of the Old England shop*, 1899, Rue Montagne de la Cour, Brussels
Archives d'Architecture Moderne, Brussels

PAUL HANKAR, *Ciamberlani residence, 1897, Rue Defacqz, Ixelles (Brussels) The garage was installed during a 1927 renovation.*

Pour la fête de sa mère, *Pathé Frères, 1906. One of the first films to show the death of a child, killed accidentally by a hunter on Mother's Day.*
Cinémathèque Royale, Brussels
Inv. 35858

CINEMA

In a very short period of time after the first public film screening (in Paris on 28 December 1895) cinema evolved from an attraction and fairground curiosity into an art based on its own fully developed language and aesthetics. Ever-growing audiences of all social strata filled the new theatres to watch images of faraway lands and peoples, and to laugh, cry or cringe in disbelief or fear at films with growingly complicated plots. The images were not only moving, they were also vividly colored and accompanied by live music (from a pianist to a full symphonic orchestra).

The reciprocal influences between cinema, considered the utmost expression of modernity, and the other arts started very early. Musicians such as Saint-Saëns wrote for the screen (one of the first to do so in 1908), actors moved freely from the theatre stage to the cinema set, the aesthetics of the private and the public sphere influenced the films and were in turn created by them, and, starting with futurism and expressionism, the link with the avant-gardes was constant. From this time on, art and cinema became inseparable.

Rendez-vous, *Max Linder, Pathé Frères, 1913*
Max meets a pretty woman and discreetly drops his handkerchief. The trap is set.
Cinémathèque Royale, Brussels
Inv. 39471

Mme Babylas aime les animaux, *Alfred Machin,*
Pathé Frères, 1911
Madame Babylas, who loves all kinds of animals, brings a pig into the house. In revenge, Monsieur Babylas goes to get a tiger.
Cinémathèque Royale, Brussels
Inv. 38263

FERNAND KHNOPFF

"The strong coherence of Khnopff's works, whether they are portraits, landscapes or purely symbolist compositions, is created by their pervasive melancholic atmosphere."

Born in 1858 into an aristocratic family of Austrian origin, Fernand Khnopff grew up in Bruges, where his father had been appointed deputy crown prosecutor. This silent, misty town had little contact with the outside world and was ignored by travellers. The memory of this lost paradise made a strong impression on the artist, who made many works on the theme, melancholic images of a past gone for ever. It was to Khnopff that the poet Georges Rodenbach naturally turned in 1892 for the design of a frontispiece for his famous short novel, *Bruges-la-Morte*. Also born in the town were Fernand's brother Georges, a future poet, and his sister Marguerite, to whom he would have an uncommon attachment all his life and who would be his only model for many years. The family later moved to Brussels, though it would take holidays in the family's country house in the village of Fosset, in the Ardennes, where the countryside inspired him to paint many works set in a strange poetic atmosphere. A solitary, melancholic adolescent, Khnopff loved literature and the legendary dreams of Gustave Flaubert, wrote verse and read poets such as Leconte de Lisle and Baudelaire, and revelled in the delights of music, a passion that never left him. He was already an artist and quickly gave up the study of the law that his father had guided him into to enter the Académie de Bruxelles, where he proved to be a more than honourable pupil. His teacher there was Xavier Mellery, in whose class he had Ensor and Deville as fellow students. Khnopff did not reject tradition as it provided him with techniques that he considered useful. He followed his Brussels training with a stay in Paris to study the masters, during which he discovered the works of Edward Burne-Jones and Gustave Moreau, who were both to have an undeniable influence on his work.

His first work was a ceiling project titled *Painting, Music, Poetry*, a thesis that encapsulated themes that would appear frequently in his later work. It was exhibited at L'Essor in 1881 where, the following year, he presented seven works that caught the attention of Émile Verhaeren. Mixing by this time with the avant-garde artistic and literary circles, in 1883 Khnopff became a founding member of Les XX (see p. 57), for which he designed the image based on its name. He would remain an active member of the group until it was dissolved ten years later, taking part in its stormy debates.

While he established himself as the preferred portraitist of the upper middle class – his portraits of children are true masterpieces of feeling and sweetness – he also undertook works inspired by literature following the example of Félicien Rops. His first symbolist image was *The Sphinx*, "Delicate, exquisite, refined, subtle, Sphinx for those who doubt all and instils doubts about all, Sphinx for the weary and the unbelievers, Sphinx for the sphinx himself", as

FERNAND KHNOPFF, **Silence,** *1890*
Pastel on paper, 87.8 × 44.3 cm
Inv. 4844

Verhaeren wrote in *L'Art moderne* in 1886. It was also at this time that Khnopff began to associate with a strange individual, Joséphin Péladan, an ardent and confused mystic, for whom Khnopff illustrated the book *Le Vice suprême*. He remained in contact with Péladan for many years and participated in four of the Salons de la Rose-Croix organized by the 'Sâr'. In 1897, tired of the guru's antics, he cut the ties between them. However, he did not dispense with the influence that Péladan had cast over him, which had helped him to formulate his idealist conceptions of art. This influence was complemented just as powerfully by that of the British Pre-Raphaelites, Edward Burne-Jones, Dante Gabriel Rossetti and George Frederic Watts, all visionary artists with whom he had close dealings from the 1890s.

The strong coherence of Khnopff's works, whether they are portraits, landscapes or purely symbolist compositions, is created by their pervasive melancholic atmosphere. Their recurrent themes are dreams, memory, flight from the world, and the apotheosis of the soul towards the Ideal. But the artist's self does not surrender itself up directly. It takes the long way round, passing through symbols, enigmas, the bizarre and occasionally the disquieting, as though passing behind screens whose purpose is to protect it. During his lifetime, Khnopff was vigilant to ensure the world would only perceive a carefully tended image of himself: a characteristic of this was his controlled even haughty behaviour, something noted by all his contemporaries. In 1886, when Khnopff was twenty-eight, Émile Verhaeren remarked that Khnopff 'considers more than he speaks', and 'observes more than he explains', and concluded, 'Stiff posture, correct behaviour, very unpretentious. A clergyman in the process of becoming a dandy.' Proud of his background and knowledge, Khnopff never ceased to cultivate the difference between himself and others; he was far from vulgar, and anxious to keep up his personal standards.

It is therefore possible to understand the obsessional recurrence of certain mythical figures in the work of this introvert, such as the Sphinx – the image of enigma as well as being the heraldic symbol of his family – and Hypnos, the god of sleep and dreaming, the space in which the impulsions of the unconscious are expressed, where the boundary between the past and the present is abolished, and where thought and creativeness unfurl. Equally haunting, the face of his sister Marguerite reappears again and again on all supports, whether alone or

FERNAND KHNOPFF, The Abandoned Town, *1904*
Pastel and crayon on paper mounted on canvas,
76 × 69 cm. Inv. 7030

associated with some symbolic motif like a flower, a wing or a mirror. Omnipresent in Khnopff's works, the artist sometimes utilizes the female figure as an allegory of silence or interiority, sometimes of decadence and the basest matter. A poet as much as a painter, Khnopff plays with colours like words, creating harmonious associations in which blue has pride of place. In the house he built for himself in 1902, he designed an interior in which only three colours were permitted: blue, white and gold. Black was used only on the doors and windows on the outside, so as to protect his citadel, the self by which he was held voluntary prisoner.

FERNAND KHNOPFF, **Listening to Schumann,** *1883*
Oil on canvas, 101.5 × 116.5 cm
Inv. 6366

A lady – the artist's mother – is seated in an armchair
in an elegant living room listening with concentration
to a piano discreetly suggested by a hand and a musical
score. In homage to Schumann, Khnopff's favourite
composer, the atmosphere suggested is one of fervour
in an attempt to transpose music, the most abstract
expression of art and a symbol of an interior life,
into visual art.

FERNAND KHNOPFF, The Sphinx *or* The Caresses, *1896*
Oil on canvas, 50.5 × 151 cm
Inv. 6768

Set against a landscape with blue columns and cabalistic
inscriptions, we see a sphinx – which, in mythology, would ask
a riddle and have the power of life and death over those who
attempted to answer it – and a young man. Leaning towards
the enticing face of the sphinx, he seems undecided: should he
surrender to the call of the flesh, of matter? But his right hand
holds a sceptre, the emblem of power, adorned with a pair of
blue wings, those of Hypnos, the god of sleep and dreams.

< FERNAND KHNOPFF, **An Angel**, *1889*
Platen photograph enhanced with coloured crayons,
29.5 × 18.4 cm
Inv. 4177

FERNAND KHNOPFF, **Memories**, *1889*   >>
Pastel on paper mounted on canvas, 127 × 200 cm
Inv. 3528

The painting is explained by its title: each of the women shown is an instant of the past. The woman in white is the only one who seems 'real', who recalls successive states of her self. To create this large pastel, Khnopff used six photographs of his sister Marguerite, an enthusiastic tennis player, in different poses. This pastel was hung on the wall of the blue room in the house he had built in 1902, where he liked to meditate or listen to music. A tennis racket that had belonged to Marguerite stood on a base in front of the painting, creating a sort of altar. Khnopff made great use of photographs. When preparing his paintings, he sometimes staged scenes with models and accessories, which he then photographed himself. When he reached the painting stage, he sometimes altered the composition. Another method he used was to photograph his paintings, and then rework the negatives by highlighting them with pastel, crayon or chalk.

FERNAND KHNOPFF

105

FERNAND KHNOPFF

OPERA

"Painters, poets, writers and musicians ranged themselves under the banner of the 'Ideal' and elected Wagner at their head."

In the prosperous Belgium of the 1860s, music found its way into the life of the bourgeoisie, and the Théâtre de la Monnaie, newly built by Joseph Poelaert, became one of the meeting places of polite society. Performances of music in Brussels were like that of other European capitals, mixing ambitious works with more entertaining pieces, operas with operettas for the public at large. The theatre alternated between Italian bel canto, grand opera and French comic opera. The evening of 22 March 1870 was a defining moment, when the crowd was able to make its judgement on the most controversial composer in Europe, Richard Wagner. For the first time in Brussels, one of his operas – *Lohengrin* – was staged in its full length. This event even attracted celebrities from Paris, such as Judith Gautier, Catulle Mendes and Villiers de l'Isle-Adam. The event was a triumph, to the extent that it has been said that Wagner caused 'an aesthetic riot that lasted thirty years'.

For many members of the audience, Wagner's work was a new experience but in music circles the composer was not unknown. Back in 1850 Charles-Louis Hanssens, the then director of the Théâtre de la Monnaie, had wished to stage *Lohengrin* but the negotiations had come to nothing. Ten years later Wagner had visited the theatre in person to direct two concerts of his music before travelling to Paris in March 1861 where, the victim of staged protests, his *Tannhaüser* was one of the bitterest failures of his career. From that time on, the composer remained resentful towards France but in Brussels enthusiasm for his works never abated, with the result that after Lohengrin, the Théâtre de la Monnaie created productions of *The Flying Dutchman* (1872) and *Tannhaüser* (1873). During the same period, a small group of Wagner fanatics was created, who decided to go to the first festival at Bayreuth, held in August 1876. On their return, they worked incessantly at organizing concerts and musical transcriptions of Wagner's works. Around 1875, when the opponents to the new music had dwindled to a minority, the public had achieved the necessary maturity to receive the German composer's full repertoire. The phenomenal success of *Lohengrin*, which was staged once more in 1878, provided a resounding confirmation of the triumph of Wagner's dramas. The theatre then underwent renovation to put on productions of the composer's 'total works of art' and Brussels was able to boast that it had taken Paris' place as the European capital of Wagnerism. The staging of *Parsifal*, which opened on 2 January 1914, represented the apogee of a trend that had begun fifty years earlier. If the expression 'symbolist Monnaie' could be used

JEAN DELVILLE, **Tristan and Isolde** (detail), *1887*
Crayon, black chalk, charcoal on paper,
44.3 × 74.4 cm
Inv. 7927

GÉO VERBANCK, **Brunhilde**, *1908*
Head, bronze and marble,
46 × 29 × 40 cm
Belfius Banque Collection, Brussels
Inv. 13400

to describe the period from 1880 to 1914, it is due to the productions staged and the artistic atmosphere of the period. Painters, poets, writers and musicians ranged themselves under the banner of the 'Ideal' and elected Wagner at their head.

Nowhere else over that thirty-year period had it been possible to hear such an omnibus of symbolist operas, including *Hérodiade* by Massenet (1881), *Sigurd* and *Salammbô* by Reyer (1884 and 1890), and *Le Roi Arthus* by Chausson (1903) to mention just a few, to which could be added new productions of works like Debussy's *Pelléas et Mélisande* (1907) and *Ariane et Barbe-Bleue* by Dukas (1909). Flanking these, the Théâtre de la Monnaie staged a series of revivals of masterpieces from the past by Gluck, Mozart and Weber, which Wagner had studied preparatory to his revision of lyrical drama.

Among the regular opera goers at the Théâtre de la Monnaie was Fernand Khnopff, a connoisseur of the Wagnerian world. His friendship with Maurice Kufferath, the theatre's director, gave Khnopff the chance to try his hand at stage design. His first attempt was made for *Le Roi Arthus* in 1903, for which he designed costumes and made sketches for the sets. In subsequent years he worked regularly with the theatre until 1914, but though his work is attested by biographers and a few surviving sketches, the lack of archives means that we cannot know all the costumes and sets he designed. It is probably that Khnopff was above all an artistic advisor to the theatre's director.

Another important innovation of the time was the greater importance attributed to fixed tableaux over the physical movement of the singers, as was the case in the production of Gluck's *Orphée et Eurydice* in 1893. As idealist operas do not evolve, they are set in a fixed time. Similarly, the characters, whether mythical or legendary, are not elements of a chronological development but of a universal context. The approaching end of the nineteenth century undermined public confidence in continual progress, and the hope for a glorious future gave way to pessimism that the end of the world was looming.

CONSTANTIN MEUNIER, **The Valkyrie,** *1898*
Equestrian statuette, bronze,
55.5 × 36.3 × 24.4 cm
Inv. 10000 / 80

HENRY DE GROUX, Ride of the Valkyries, c. *1890*
Pastel on paper, mounted on thick cardboard,
79.4 × 112.2 cm
Inv. 12.075

JEAN DELVILLE, Tristan and Isolde, *1887*
Crayon, black chalk, charcoal on paper,
44.3 × 74.4 cm
Inv. 7927

RICHARD WAGNER, Parsifal
New production staged in French
at the Théâtre de la Monnaie, 2 January 1914
The enchanted garden of Klingsor (Act II, scene 1)
Jean Delescluze, set designer
Model, facsimile 3PMuseum
La Monnaie – De Munt, Brussels

ERNEST REYER, Salammbô
World première at the Théâtre de la Monnaie,
10 February 1890
The feast of the mercenaries in Hamilcar's
garden (Act 1)
Pierre Devis & Armand Lynen, set designers
Model of the set, facsimile 3PMuseum
La Monnaie – De Munt, Brussels

FERNAND KHNOPFF, Mélisande, *undated*
Pastel and coloured crayon on paper, 33 × 33 cm
Inv. 12.273

JEAN DELVILLE, Orpheus Dead, *1893* >
Oil on canvas (remounted), 73.3 × 99.2 cm
Inv. 12209

In March 1893 the Théâtre de la Monnaie staged Gluck's opera
Orphée et Eurydice, whose Greek mythological hero was
frequently represented in symbolist iconography. Through
his beautiful music, this bard, who had been initiated into the
Dionysian mysteries, was able to charm all living creatures and
even stones, but he was torn to pieces by maenads and his head
thrown into the river. Jean Delville (1867–1953) became fascinated
in turn by the legend he saw performed at the Opera. In this
painting, the hero is shown as an androgynous being whose
long hair is framed by a lyre floating on the water, while a
supernatural light bathes his face. His eyes are closed,
symbolizing interiority and mystery.

MELISANDE

ARTHUR CRACO, Medusa, *undated*
Low relief head, ivory and bronze, 24 × 37 × 9.5 cm
Inv. 11362

CHRYSELEPHANTINE SCULPTURE

The controversial question of the annexation of the Congo by Belgium from the personal control of Léopold II led the king to show his subjects the interest of the territory, in particular its ivory resources, which had already made Antwerp a world market in this precious material. Consequently, a section dedicated to the Congo was mounted in Tervueren as part of the 1897 International Exposition, which attracted both the public at large as well as art lovers. The main room, designed by Paul Hankar, held eighty ivory and gold sculptures executed by thirty or so artists. The participants included Charles Samuel; Julien Dillens; Fernand Khnopff, who presented a mask; and Charles van der Stappen, whose Sphinx, a helmeted and armoured woman, was inspired by Athena. The event had an effect on both artists and public, and the production of ivory sculpture in fin-de-siècle Belgium developed greatly, resulting in several remarkable works.

Tervueren exhibition, 1897. Photograph by Alexandre
Musée Royal de l'Afrique Centrale, Tervueren. Inv. HP 1960.5.1603

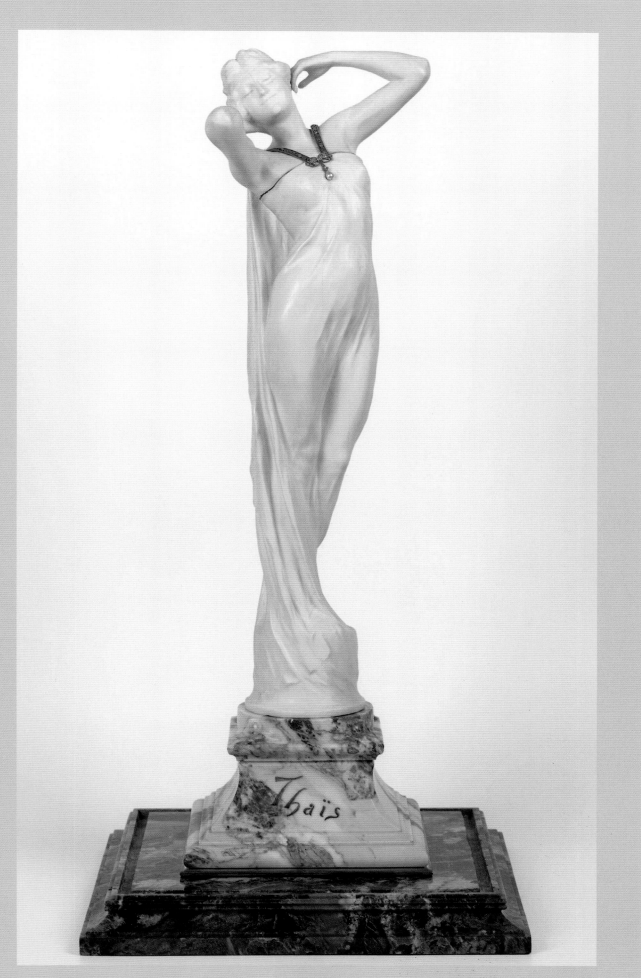

GODEFROID DEVREESE, Thaïs,
pre-1899
Statuette, ivory, gold necklace
with diamonds and a pearl;
gold bracelet, marble base,
41.5 × 17.5 × 29.5 cm
Inv. 11377

SYMBOLISM

"Rejection of materialism and all those who justified it philosophically, rejection of a world that progress was defiling and making ugly, and rejection of the aesthetics that celebrated that reality, such as naturalism."

Rather than a precisely defined movement, symbolism was more an artistic current that, in the late nineteenth century, found outlets in literature, painting and music. It is customary to attribute its birth to 1886, when the French poet Jean Moréas published his *Manifeste*, which contained a key phrase that described symbolism's aims: 'To clothe the Ideal in material form.' In Brussels the same year, *L'Art moderne* spread awareness of his premise and explained, 'Nature seen through temperament is the famous formula of naturalism. Temperament seen through nature, and even without nature, must, it seems, be the formula of innovators.' And, in answer to the question of whether the Real or the Subjective should be given precedence, the article added, 'Symbolism replies: Nature should only serve as an accessory to convey the dreams of the brain.'

The placing of greater importance on the ideal than the material had in fact occurred much earlier in other forms, for example, in romanticism, of which symbolism was a later manifestation of sorts, and again in the works of Baudelaire, whose visionary poetry remained a powerful reference for later generations, Félicien Rops in particular. Like romanticism, symbolism – and the stance taken by the artists and writers who were members of this loose conglomeration during the 1880s – was based on rupture and rejection: rejection of materialism and all those who justified it philosophically, rejection of a world that progress was defiling and making ugly, and rejection of the aesthetics that celebrated that reality, such as naturalism. From that time, praise was heaped on anything that echoed the idealist and mystical tradition, such as the works of writers as varied as Swedenborg and Schopenhauer, with the French translation of the latter's *The World as Will and Representation* making a profound impact in France and Belgium. The helplessness and despondency experienced by van de Velde, Max

JEAN DELVILLE, **Mysteriosa**, *1892*
Crayon, pastel and coloured crayons on paper, 40 × 32.1 cm
Inv. 12029

Radiating light, the face of this woman is reduced to a pair of unseeing eyes: they are gazing elsewhere, into an invisible world beyond our perception. Her long, diaphanous hands rest on a book whose cover is stamped with a triangle, the symbol of the Holy Trinity. Her chin resting on the book is a clear invitation to us to place our faith in God in order to evade darkness and doubt.

ODILON REDON, **Christ**, *1878 or 1880*
Charcoal and black chalk on paper,
34.2 × 27.2 cm
Inv. 7951

FÉLICIEN ROPS, **Le Vice suprême**, *1884*
Graphite, Indian ink and highlights in white gouache on paper, 23.8 × 16 cm
Inv. 11996

>>

EDWARD BURNE-JONES, **Psyche's Wedding**, *1895*
Oil on canvas, 119.5 × 215.5 cm
Inv. 7350

This painting illustrates an episode from the *Marriage of Cupid and Psyche* by Apuleius (second century): forced by her father to marry a monster – which later turns out to be Cupid – Psyche is led by a procession of young girls towards her dreaded spouse. The night-time setting, the elegance and refinement of the figures, and the frieze-like composition make this late painting one of the Pre-Raphaelite artist's most beautiful works.

Elskamp and Maurice Maeterlinck are indicative of the crisis that artists and writers of the period in general were undergoing. However, personal doubt did not slow their creativity but in fact seemed to stimulate it, if we are to judge by the famous *Confession de poète* published by Émile Verhaeren in *L'Art moderne* in 1890, in which he adopted the motto, '*Se torturer savamment*', which might be translated as 'Torture yourself with care.'

Mobilization of the symbolists against the prevailing positivism took many forms, notably through the drawing to attention of such unconventional figures as androgynes, madmen and clowns, or by acclaiming elements suggestive of the inexpressible, such as water, plants, the unconscious and death. In order to escape the oppressiveness of daily life, some created an enclosed world for themselves, such as Maurice Maeterlinck with *Les Serres chaudes* and Georges Rodenbach with *Les Vies encloses*, while in the pictorial domain Odilon Redon chose to take refuge in dream and Xavier Mellery drew mysterious interiors as an expression of the poetry of silence – works in which the subconscious expressed itself, sometimes not at the artist's bidding. In 1891 Maeterlinck offered a definition of symbolism in which he noted the role of the subconscious in creativity: 'The poet must, it seems to me, be passive in [the use of] a symbol, and the purest symbol is perhaps the one that appears independent of his knowledge and even his design.'

Those who withdrew into themselves were countered by artists who likened themselves to initiates imbued with a truth to be transmitted to their fellowmen. Presented in a disguised form, the truth in question was for contemplation, as was advocated by Sâr Péladan, who assigned art the task of incarnating Ideal Beauty. Members of the symbolist current adopted very different individual stances and expressed themselves in a very different manner, allowing such dissimilar groups as the Pre-Raphaelites, School of Pont-Aven, Nabis, neo-impressionists, idealists and luminists – taking England, Belgium and France alone into consideration – to be grouped under the same banner. These were joined by, or sometimes improperly associated with, some artists who blazed a personal trail.

It is however possible to discern several major themes that were sufficiently recurrent in symbolism to be significant and to recognize those individuals who exemplified the rejection of the contemporary world. The flight from modernity was at times represented by a return to the past, to a Golden Age or idealized Middle Ages, thus from the 1860s Edward Burne-Jones, under the influence of Dante Gabriele Rossetti, the founder of the first Pre-Raphaelite movement, developed a passion for the Italian Primitives. His refined oeuvre presents figures inspired by Botticelli in settings permeated by melancholy or nostalgia. When symbolists did not draw their inspiration from history, they often turned instead to myth: fin-de-siècle iconography abounds in figures like Prometheus, Icarus and Orpheus, all borrowed from ancient mythology, as well as from characters from the world of Wagner, such as the many Tristans and Isoldes, Parsifals and Valkyries. Biblical and Christian traditions were another source, providing the figures of Salome, Judith, Saint Anthony and Christ. But symbolist artists did not simply present the 'history painting' typical of the classical ages or of contemporary academic painters: the goal was to give material form to an idea, or to a personal and poetic aspiration. What was important in revisiting these ancient themes was to share a dream, or to express a form of suffering or anguish. These insubstantial sentiments and sensations could only be conveyed through the use of symbols.

That was the undertaking that art critic Albert Aurier ascribed to symbolist artists when he wrote in 1891: 'The work of art must be, firstly, '*ideational*'; secondly, *symbolistic*, because it expresses an idea in forms; thirdly, *synthetic*, because it describes these forms and signs in a generally understandable way; fourthly, *objective*, because the object is never considered an object per se but rather as a sign for an idea that is expressed through the object; fifthly, *decorative*.'

One of the 'objects' most commonly used by symbolist painters was the mirror, which was so frequent in the works of Khnopff, Spilliaert and Redon that it might be made the emblem of the symbolist current. They used it as a pretext for the questioning of the self and identity, a means to express the fragile boundary that exists between reality and

FÉLICIEN ROPS, The Temptation of Saint Anthony, *1878*
Pastel, 73.7 × 54.4 cm
Bibliothèque Royale de Belgique, Brussels
This drawing, which was exhibited at the first Salon des XX in 1884, has strong affinities with Rops' *Sataniques*, a series of strongly anticlerical works. Christ has been substituted on the cross by a voluptuous woman and the traditional INRI has been replaced by the inscription EROS. Deep in meditation, Saint Anthony is surprised by this apparition and abruptly looks up from his study. The image represents the powerlessness of faith faced by the incitement of the senses. The work's first owner was Edmond Picard, one of the founders of Les XX.

unreality, life and death (introspective functions also found in self-portraiture), and most importantly an instrument to express the solitude of man in a universe not under his command.

However, rejection of the reality of the contemporary world does not always equate with a denial of its existence. It is also possible to protest against its faults, its vices and its perversions, or to point out its evil ways. This is what Félicien Rops did in his customary corrosive manner when he painted *The Temptation of Saint Anthony* to stigmatize the sexual hypocrisy of his age, and in his illustrations for *Le Vice suprême*, the novel in which Sâr Péladan described the struggle undertaken by secret forces to destroy humanity. As the Devil is everywhere, he makes use of invisible armies and messengers from the underworld that we need to recognize beneath their attractive guise. One of these is a woman, a dangerous temptress whose only task is to lead men into disgrace and ruin despite her promises of voluptuous pleasure. This is the premise of Jean Delville's painting *Satan's Treasures*, but examples are legion.

A painter, as well as a poet and essayist, Jean Delville was an important figure in Belgian symbolism. His aim, which was broadly stimulated by Péladan's Rosicrucian theories, was to transform society by presenting it with a form of wisdom that mixed esotericism, Neoplatonism and a theosophical utopia, in which the individual's soul is guided by astral light, 'the second state of substance and a great magnetic reservoir of undefined forces'. In this fluid universe, each form and colour is permeated by a mysterious force whose source is God, contemplation of which leads to ecstasy. Striving for the absolute, Delville stripped the figures of their 'accidental' existence and focused on the dematerialization of their bodies, the evanescence of colour, and the radiation of an astral light. The writhing flesh, contorted bodies and insubstantial faces are suggestive of morbid abandonment. The painter published all his theories together in 1900 in *La Mission de l'art* prefaced by Édouard Schuré, the author of *Les grands initiés*.

Some painters, such as Albert Ciamberlani, Émile Fabry and Constant Montald, followed his idealist path for a while before shifting their attention to the decorative possibilities these themes offered. In Montald's works, the figures are integrated into the landscape among graceful vegetation, unrealistic decorative effects, and highly mannered lighting effects that fall within the art nouveau aesthetic. As from 1897 Montald was to produce a great many monumental works.

LÉON SPILLIAERT,
Maurice Maeterlinck.
Les Serres chaudes.
Album, *1918*
Ten lithographs inspired by Maurice Maeterlinck's Les Serres chaudes, *embellished by the artist. Artist's proof. Lithograph, Indian ink wash, coloured crayon on paper, 49 × 36.7 cm Inv. 12154*

Bookbinding by Paul Claessens made after the artwork by Henry van de Velde, 1897
Cover in ivory parchment with gilt decoration on the coat of arms of Léopold II, ruler of the Congo Free State (1885–1908), with the motto "TRAVAIL ET PROGRÈS". Lined in yellowed watered silk. 38.1 × 26.5 cm
Bibliotheca Wittockiana, Brussels

ART NOUVEAU BOOKBINDING

Having given up easel painting in order to devote himself to a 'social' art that would involve him more in everyday life, Henry van de Velde (1863–1957) investigated all the different types of decorative art. Between 1893 and 1900, he designed twenty or so book bindings, including the blocking stamps that his binder in Brussels, Paul Claessens, commissioned from a workshop in Paris (Béarel & Cie). Sometimes made for his own library, these bindings were also made for individual purchasers, including Léopold II of Belgium. One of them, designed for a document holder in ivory-coloured parchment, bears the coat of arms of the Congo Free State embellished with a mosaic of coloured leather and accompanied by the motto 'Travail et Progrès'. All of van de Velde's cover designs are based on patterns of undulating lines characteristic of art nouveau. Increasingly stylised, the floral decoration developed from figurative to linear representations.

WILLY SCHLOBACH, Death / Ophelia, *1890*
Pastel on paper, 62 × 183 cm
Archives et Musée de la Littérature,
Bibliothèque Royale de Belgique, Brussels
Deposited with the Musées royaux des Beaux-Arts de Belgique
Inv. PT/TB KB 2002

WILLIAM DEGOUVE DE NUNCQUES, The Peacocks, *1896*
Pastel on paper mounted on canvas, 59.5 × 99 cm
Inv. 9397

Self-taught, Degouve de Nuncques (1867–1935) was an
instinctive painter, claiming that, to make a painting, it was
enough to draw the lines and fill in the rest with feelings. During
his pre-1900 symbolist period, he had a fondness for mysterious
night scenes bathed in blue that prefigured surrealism. To
him, colour was not a goal in itself but a means of expressing
emotion.

JEAN DELVILLE, Satan's Treasures, *1895*
Oil on canvas, 258 × 268 cm
Inv. 4575

Won over to Sâr Péladan's esoteric teachings, Delville
(1867–1953) focused his art more on evocation than
description. This swarm of women determined to drag
man down into the watery depths is an invitation to us
to free ourselves from the demands of the flesh and
human passions to rise towards the immaterial.

CHARLES VAN DER STAPPEN, Sphinx, *1898*
Bust, marble, 70.5 × 56 × 34 cm
Inv. 3465

Taken from Greek mythology, the Sphinx is a frequent motif in symbolist art. An allegory of enigma, the Sphinx is a hybrid being traditionally composed of the bust of a woman and the winged body of a lion. In this sculpture the animal characteristics are reduced to the ornamentation on the helmet. The lowered eyes and closed mouth suggest secrecy, a recurrent theme at the turn of the century.

CONSTANT MONTALD, Dancing Nymphs, c. 1898
Oil and tempera on canvas, 95.5 × 135.5 cm
Inv. 8435

These graceful nymphs seem to be dancing in a sort of
Eden in which everything is suggestive of gentle harmony.
The unrealistic landscape is painted in a limited range of pale
colours inspired by the Italian Primitives and fresco painting.
In this work, symbolism is purely decorative. Montald
(1862–1944) frequently included metal particles in his
works to increase their luminosity.

CONSTANT MONTALD, The Fountain of Inspiration, *1907*
Oil on canvas, 535 × 525 cm (original dimensions);
393 × 490 cm (without stretcher)
Inv. 12105

CHUTE DES DERNIERES FEUILLES D'AUTOMNE

XAVIER MELLERY,
Fall of the Last Leaves of Autumn.
Autumn, c. *1890*
*Watercolour, ink, charcoal and
black chalk on paper mounted on
cardboard. Silver-gold ground,
92 × 59 cm*
Inv. 3913

MELLERY AND ALLEGORY

There are two different sides to Xavier Mellery's works. The better-known are his drawings of interiors in which he gives a vision of the world through the dialogue between light and shade. These interiors lit by the flame of a candle or by light seeping beneath a door are bathed in an aura of silence and introspection. The other facet of his oeuvre was decorative in nature, prompted by the frescoes in the Sistine Chapel during his stay in Rome in 1870, and influenced by the works of Puvis de Chavannes and the Pre-Raphaelites. Together these inspired him to produce numerous projects for wall decorations, featuring realist images set against a gold ground denoting the Ideal. Devised for public buildings, the aim of these allegories, most of which were never executed, was to achieve what Mellery (1845–1921) called the "modern synthesis". A founder member in 1892 of the group Pour l'Art, he participated in the last Rose–Croix exhibition in Paris with his former pupil, Fernand Khnopff.

XAVIER MELLERY,
Maternal Pride, *undated*
*Watercolour, ink and crayon on
paper mounted on cardboard.
Varnished gold ground, 76 × 58 cm*
Inv. 3578

XAVIER MELLERY, Corner of
a Church in Bruges, *undated*
Two drawings; crayon, black and
brown chalk, brush and Indian
ink, blue watercolour on paper
fully mounted on cardboard,
51.6 × 32.3 cm ; 51.9 × 32.4 cm
Inv. 3381/1-2

XAVIER MELLERY,
Effect of the Light, *undated*
Study, black chalk, Indian ink wash
on paper, 25.6 × 13.6 cm
Inv. 4458/1

THE GILLION CROWET COLLECTION

"In breaking with the canons of the past and inventing new lines on completely new themes, the baroque imagination of art nouveau had represented the modernity of the moment."

As a consequence of the donation against tax made by the Gillion Crowet family in 2006 to the Région Bruxelles-Capitale, the Musées royaux de Belgique are able to present the largest collection of art nouveau works. Given its own space in the museum, this collection offers a superb overview of a period that was particularly important in the history of the decorative arts. Previously relegated to the rank of minor arts, in the very early years of the 1900s they came to share the same aesthetic and spiritual goals as the fine arts: that of the creation of an interior as a 'total work of art' – what Émile Gallé, the master of art nouveau in Nancy, summed up with the term 'symbolist decor'. The approximately two hundred works in the Gillion Crowet collection – glassware, jewellery, sculptures, furniture, paintings – are shining examples of this ambition prevalent throughout Europe.

In breaking with the canons of the past and inventing new lines on completely new themes, the baroque imagination of art nouveau had represented the modernity of the moment. But during the twentieth century, this art was undervalued, suffered disaffection and was even rejected as being 'mannerist, decadent and decorative'. Its restoration to grace came too late to save much of the architectural heritage from the period, which had been demolished, and its decorative arts, which had suffered damaging neglect. In this belittling context typical of the 1960s – when even Victor Horta's Maison du Peuple was demolished – two young collectors fell in love with art nouveau: Anne-Marie Crowet and her husband Roland Gillion. Over a period of thirty years, Anne-Marie Crowet, herself the daughter of a great collector, scoured the sales rooms, antique dealers, flea markets and private sellers, buying, reselling and exchanging pieces

ALPHONSE MUCHA, Nature: Pagan Divinity, *1899–1900*
Sculpture, gilded bronze with malachite highlights,
executed by Émile Pinedo
H. 70 cm
Région Bruxelles-Capitale,
Deposited with the Musées royaux des Beaux-Arts de Belgique
Inv. GC 122

La Nature was cast in Paris by Émile Pinedo and is probably one of Alphonse Mucha's greatest works. Presented at the 1900 Universal Exposition in Paris, and again in Turin in 1902, it was created in four versions that differed only in their ornamentation. This exemplar is the only one to have remained entirely gilded, just as it was exhibited in 1900. The common point between the sculptures is the serenity of this divine apparition, a quality that Mucha (1860-1939) brought out with the Byzantine effect of the gleaming bronze, which idealizes the figure's skin through its luminous radiance. Drawn apart like a curtain, then together again below the bust, the figure's hair suggests that this beautiful and mysterious face is rising out of the water.

ALPHONSE MUCHA *and* ADOLPHE TRUFFIER,
La Princesse lointaine: Mask with Scarabs,
1900
Wall light, gilded and chased bronze
on a wooden support
H. 42 cm
Région Bruxelles-Capitale,
Deposited with the Musées royaux
des Beaux-Arts de Belgique
Inv. GC 081

in order to finally acquire the very best. In the late 1980s, the couple's outstanding collection included works by prestigious names including Gallé, Lalique, Majorelle, Cros, Horta and Mucha, and paintings by Khnopff, Delville, Schwabe and Mossa.

To prevent the collection from being broken up or taken abroad, the Gillion Crowet family instigated a procedure in which the collection was donated against the settling of the inheritance laws with the proviso that the public would be allowed to see this precious heritage of the identity and collective memory of Belgium. A committee was set up to oversee the fulfilment of the project, with representatives of the three parties involved – the Gillion Crowet family, the Région Bruxelles-Capitale and the Belgian Federal State – as well as Belgian and foreign experts involved in enhancing the collection. This was to pass into the care of the Musées royaux des Beaux-Arts de Belgique, whose duty it would be to make the collection available to the public at large. After a long process, the donation to the Région Bruxelles-Capitale was finally concluded. A large number of pieces was also generously donated by the Gillion Crowet family to extend the spirit of this collection in the Musée Fin-de-Siècle Museum. The joint effort, initiated privately, has allowed masterpieces of art nouveau from a family heritage to be conserved today for the benefit of future generations.

The impression received by the viewer of these art nouveau gems is of extreme refinement. All the traditional materials of the decorative arts – ceramic, glass, wood and metal – are used but have often been reworked or reformulated – all the more so as chemistry, which was advanced by this time, created unrivalled possibilities – and sometimes combined in unusual fashion. The extraordinary expertise of the glassworkers, goldsmiths, silversmiths and sculptors of the early 1900s resulted in works of unprecedented delicacy: those of the highest quality are by Émile Gallé, whose exceptional items of glassware are the result of persevering experimentation with the material, and by Henri Cros, who sculpted faces using glass paste.

Another work of outstanding quality is *La Nature*, one of the highlights of the collection, designed by Alphonse Mucha and executed by the bronze sculptor Émile Pinedo. The golden gleam of the bronze suffuses a tremor of life into the mysterious young woman with closed eyes. Another woman's face can be discerned among the masterful combination of curves on Mucha's wall light *La Princesse lointaine*, but the female figure so recurrent in the work of the symbolists also lent itself to more disturbing interpretations, as is seen in *La Méduse* by Fernand Khnopff and *Malefica* by the goldsmith Philippe Wolfers.

It is not possible to consider art nouveau without bearing in mind Japanism, one of the elements that fundamentally contributed to it. The passion for the arts of Japan among all the artists of Europe for two decades reached its pinnacle during the first decade of the twentieth century, when it powerfully influenced the style of the period. The attention paid to lines, materials, reliefs and chromatic relationships was derived from the Japanese. The themes of Japanese art were also taken up, thus, as nature was the source of all beauty in the Land of the Rising Sun, flowers and birds, plants and insects became the focus of artists in the West, developed with an increasingly diverse and refined repertoire. This background gave rise to Louis Majorelle's range of Nénuphar furniture and Antonin Daum's Magnolia lamp. And Émile Gallé, an expert on nature and a virtuoso sculptor, designed a pedestal table in which the legs are in the form of dragonflies.

The interest in craftsmanship at the turn of the century was indeed influenced by the arts of Japan and the care given to the humblest of domestic objects, but it was also derived from a tradition of longer standing, that of the English Arts and Crafts Movement which, when it rediscovered the Middle Ages in 1860, restored honour to the applied arts. Forty years later, in London, in Paris at the Arts Décoratifs, in the Vienna and Munich Secessions, in Darmstadt, one of the seats of Jugendstil, and in Brussels, all artists, working with the most diverse materials, applied themselves to introducing beauty into daily life. The paintings of the symbolists were very much at home in this new environment, as they, too, offered an escape from reality into fantasy.

PHILIPPE WOLFERS, Malefica, *1905*
Sculpture, red marble (porphyry) worked so that the veins in the stone correspond to the veins beneath the skin, ivory for the serpents in the hair adorned with amethyst; the mask is in the same style as a jewel made by the artist in 1898, H. 61.5 cm
Région Bruxelles-Capitale,
Deposited with the Musées royaux des Beaux-Arts de Belgique
Inv. GC 124

ÉMILE GALLÉ, *Dragonfly pedestal table, first version, 1900 (and detail)*
Three-legged pedestal table in walnut with image of a marshy landscape created with marquetry and mother-of-pearl inlay, 75.5 × 59 cm
Région Bruxelles-Capitale, Deposited with the Musées royaux des Beaux-Arts de Belgique
Inv. GC 151

LOUIS MAJORELLE, *Nénuphar ladies' desk,*
c. 1903 (and detail)
Sculpted mahogany decorated with
moulding, marquetry and gilded bronze,
98 × 130.5 × 80 cm
Région Bruxelles-Capitale,
Deposited with the Musées royaux
des Beaux-Arts de Belgique
Inv. GC 139

LOUIS MAJORELLE, *Nénuphar desk chair, c. 1903*
Mahogany and (original) leather decorated with
Nénuphar gilded bronze fittings, 87 × 73 × 77.8 cm
Région Bruxelles-Capitale,
Deposited with the Musées royaux
des Beaux-Arts de Belgique
Inv. GC 158

ÉMILE GALLÉ, Sea Horses, c. 1901–1903
Blown glass in several layers, metal inclusions and applications,
surface engraving, and patina created by oxide fumes, 18 × 14.5 cm
Artist's double line signature and date engraved on the lower
section of the belly: GALLÉ
Région Bruxelles-Capitale,
Deposited with the Musées royaux des Beaux-Arts de Belgique
Inv. GC 001

A masterpiece by Émile Gallé (1846–1904), this vase is an example of
the evolution of the artist towards creating a sculptural effect. He made
several versions of this same vase between 1901 and 1903. This one
was exhibited in March 1903 at the Exposition Lorraine held at the Musée
des Art Décoratifs. The pieces of coral, acid burns, effects of the light,
alternation between roughness and smoothness, and the skilfully created
irregularity of form are all indicative of the technical mastery achieved
by Gallé at the end of his life.

HENRI and DÉSIRÉ MULLER,
Two cylindrical vases with slightly swollen bodies,
1906–07
Two layers, etched and engraved with hydrofluoric
acid, enamel decoration metallized by oxide fumes,
41 × 13 cm; 41.3 × 11.8 cm
Cristallerie du Val Saint-Lambert, Seraing
Région Bruxelles-Capitale,
Deposited with the Musées royaux
des Beaux-Arts de Belgique
Inv. GC 056

PHILIPPE WOLFERS, Orchid, *1894*
Jardinière in solid silver, with floral pattern rim,
41 × 30 × 37 cm
Région Bruxelles-Capitale,
Deposited with the Musées royaux
des Beaux-Arts de Belgique
Inv. GC 113

Towards modernity
Lines and forms

LÉON SPILLIAERT

"His images go straight to the essence, excluding trivial details and conventional ornamentation. Views that stretch for ever and vast empty spaces emphasize man's solitude and infinite sadness."

Born in Ostend, where his father was a perfumer that supplied, among others, the court of Léopold II, in 1881, Léon Spilliaert was an introverted youngster whose complex psychological make-up went hand in hand with his precarious health. He spent a brief period at the Académie de Bruges in 1899, where he studied "ancient heads", but his spontaneous and precocious talents as a draughtsman gained nothing by this training and he may be considered self-taught. At the age of twenty-two, this lover of literature – who had read Nietzsche, Poe, Lautréamont and the symbolist poets and who was himself a writer – was offered a job in Brussels by the publisher Edmond Deman. This was his opportunity: Deman was an art lover whose walls were hung with works by Ensor, Lemmen, Khnopff and van Rysselberghe, but he also had an important collection of lithographs by Odilon Redon that made a strong impression on the young Spilliaert. In addition, Deman introduced him to the symbolist literary circles in the city, and when Spilliaert wanted to try his luck in Paris in 1904, Deman sent him to Émile Verhaeren. The pair quickly struck up a strong friendship and the poet purchased a few of Spilliaert's works. He also put him in contact with the members of the art world, which allowed Spilliaert to exhibit his works, though to no great success. Thus he returned to Ostend, where he remained until the outbreak of war.

This was the period of his most surprising works, executed using watercolours, gouaches, coloured crayons, pastels and ink, often combined. Indian ink in particular, which he handled with rare delicacy, allowed him to create atmospheres that are both mysterious and tragic. He took his subjects from the world around him, such as the seafront, the port, the sea walls, the landing stage, and the streets of Ostend and its surrounding area, which he walked alone at night. At times taking geometric perspective to the limits of abstraction, he had a marked preference for night scenes that enabled him to express his melancholic side. People are not absent from all his oeuvre, nor himself as he made odd self-portraits in which he seems racked by anxiety and the questioning of his "*moi dramatique*", or anima, which Edvard Munch was exploring at the same moment. Sometimes he painted fishermen, women with haunted expressions or solitary figures seen from behind in empty spaces. But Spilliaert also made humorous sketches of bathers on the beach, like his fellow townsman James Ensor. Another genre he tackled was still lifes, with mirrors and green plants as recurrent motifs, or he might also restrict his subject to a single object, such as a small bottle or simple dish.

Unconcerned by realism, Spilliaert included art nouveau motifs such as arabesques, Japanizing decorative flat tints, and contrasting colours. His images go straight to the essence, excluding trivial details and conventional ornamentation. Views that stretch for ever and vast empty spaces emphasize man's solitude and infinite sadness and denote Spilliaert as a member of the symbolist current. However, like van de Velde, his interpretation of his subject matter was that of a modernist, marked by a concern for the clarity and sharpness of his lines and for the precision of his treatment.

In 1916 Léon Spilliaert married Rachel Vergison and the following year the couple moved to Brussels. This development represented a new page in the artist's career, one in which his output was less original and of varying quality. To support his family, he produced a great many watercolours and gouaches that he knocked off in short time, of assorted motifs but especially seascapes of unusual tonalities and featuring horizontal bands. Angst gave way to humour, intimism and nonchalance.

Fiercely independent, Spilliaert did not associate himself with any school or group with a stated aim. Only a few enlightened art lovers and poets seems to have understood his work during his lifetime. He long remained unknown to the Belgian public and ignored abroad before being rediscovered during the 1980s, when he was granted important exhibitions in Belgium and round the world.

LÉON SPILLIAERT, **The Sea Wall**, *1909*
Brush and Indian ink wash, watercolour, coloured crayon on folded paper mounted on cardboard, 99.8 × 73.8 cm
Inv. 10224
One of Spilliaert's favourite motifs was the sea, always close at hand, unvarying yet changing like one's moods. It is seen here in a striking design in which a powerful diagonal leads the eye towards the horizon. Dark and light areas contrast strongly, as do the curves and straight lines. In this deserted space the only allusions to humanity are given by the hut and luminous haloes of the lighthouses.

LÉON SPILLIAERT, **Self-Portrait**, *1907*
Watercolour, Indian ink and coloured crayon on paper,
48.8 × 63 cm
Inv. 6923

This self-portrait emanates an aura of 'worrying strangeness' very typical of Spilliaert's production of the time. Reflected in a mirror with dark, hollow eye sockets, his head appears like a skull, an image that betrays the artist's malaise and his questioning of reality.

LÉON SPILLIAERT, Bather, *1910*
Brush and Indian ink, pastel on paper,
64.9 × 50.4 cm
Inv. 6622

The art of the Nabis is called
irresistibly to mind by this *Bather*
by its cropped framing and use of
a low angle perspective, but also
by the mischievous note represented
by the dog. And in a similar Nabi
spirit, Spilliaert contrasts the geometric
mass of the steps in the foreground
with the Japanizing swirls on the
water's surface.

LÉON SPILLIAERT, Boxes in Front of a Mirror, c. *1904*
Pastel, charcoal on paper mounted on cardboard,
58.5 × 40.1 cm
Inv. 4898

The unusual subject of this work, a modern version of
the Renaissance 'vanities', is a reminder that Léon Spilliaert's
father had a perfumery, La Grande Parfumerie Spilliaert–
Jonckheere. Boxes and bottles were therefore part of the
artist's everyday existence since his early childhood. Here
they are placed in front of a mirror, which both doubles
their presence whilst also dematerializing them; beneath
the glass dome in the background, we make out a clock
without hands, an explicit symbol of death.

LÉON SPILLIAERT, Galeries royales d'Ostende, *1908* >>
Indian ink wash and pen, coloured crayon on
paper, 31.7 × 49.9 cm
Inv. 6621

THE SCHOOL OF SINT-MARTENS-LATEM GEORGE MINNE

"Two generations of artists whose common point was their rejection of the progress imposed by modernist ideology, which they countered with a rural ideal tinged with archaism and melancholy. "

Standing on the banks of the River Lys not far from Ghent, the village of Sint-Martens-Latem harboured two generations of artists whose common point was their rejection of the progress imposed by modernist ideology, which they countered with a rural ideal tinged with archaism and melancholy. The colony developed into a community known in particular for its passage from symbolism to expressionism. The "first Latem group", as it is conventionally called, included the designer and sculptor George Minne, and the painters Valerius de Saedeleer, Gustave van de Woestyne and Albert Servaes. The second group was essentially represented by Gustave de Smet, Constant Permeke and Frits van den Berghe, who are generally thought of as the initiators of Flemish expressionism.

When George Minne settled in Latem in 1899, at the age of thirty-six, he had already created a large body of work and was not unknown in literary and art circles. His career began early as in 1886, very shortly after he left the Ghent art academy, he sculpted the moving *Mother Weeping over Her Dead Child*, in which he melded the two themes of motherhood

and death in a vision of synthesis to which he would remain faithful. During the same year he got to know the poet Grégoire Le Roy, also from Ghent, whom he introduced to Émile Verhaeren and Maurice Maeterlinck. These three were to play a key role in Minne's career, defending the artist against those who criticized his awkward manner and rudimentary execution. In 1890 Le Roy devoted an important article to Minne's work in *L'Art moderne*, writing: "It is the infinite and eternal dimensions of human suffering that M. Georges Minne discloses to us in a symbol and impresses upon us powerfully." Verhaeren published a laudatory article in *La Nation* the following year, but it was with Maeterlinck that Minne had the warmest relationship, which materialized in a close partnership. The writer – who called Minne "the great portrayer of sorrow" – asked him to illustrate his book of poems *Serres chaudes* (1899) and his three plays *La Princesse Maleine* (1899), *Alladine et Palomides* (1894) and *Soeur Béatrice* (1900). Drawn in a very personal style, they are not unlike medieval woodcuts, as the poet perfectly realized: "Georges Minne is a direct descendant of the admirable Flemish artists from the Burgundian age. . . . He does not imitate them in the slightest, he is naturally like them, they are spontaneously returned to life in him."

Minne showed his works in public for the first time at the Triennial Salon in Ghent in 1889 and, at Verhaeren's suggestion, a year later he was invited to exhibit with Les XX. In 1892 he was elected a member

GEORGE MINNE, **The Small Relic Bearer,** *1897*
Kneeling statue, marble, 67 × 18.5 × 38 cm
Inv. 4789

The contemplative, sorrowful, gaunt kneeling figure is fully engrossed in himself. By simplifying to the extreme, Minne (1866–1941) succeeded in giving his sculptures a dimension of monumentality. Borrowing the theme of the repetition of identical figures from Rodin, the master he admired, in 1900 Minne created a composition in which five Kneeling Figures were placed around a circular fountain.

of the group when he was twenty-six years old. Following a short attempt to live in the countryside, Minne left for Brussels where for a year he attended a sculpture course given by Charles van der Stappen. This marked the start of a period of intense production in which he created some of his most significant works: *The Kneeling Youth, The Prodigal Son* (1896), *The Small Relic Bearer* (1897) and the *Fountain with Kneeling Youths* (1898), which Minne would exhibit at La Libre Esthétique. The art of this introverted and anguished sculptor is surprisingly stark, and characterized in particular by the importance of the lines and the obsessional repetition of certain figures, such as those of the mother and, above all, the kneeling youth, who represents the fragility of man crushed by a fate over which none of us has control, and who is condemned to meditate on his condition. Like Minne, Albert Servaes spent most of his life in Latem, living there at the same time as Frits van den Berghe and Gustave van de Woestyne, he was attached to both groups and served as the stylistic link between the two. From 1905, his rural and religious scenes mingled the most extreme forms of symbolism and expressionism. His early, very dark paintings, often of strangely lit night scenes, are intensely mystical yet, at the same time, are the first explicit expression of one of the major messages, which they convey harshly and powerfully, of Flemish expressionism – the close relationship of man and the land.

The cohesion of the group in terms of ideas and sensibility was founded on the literary and philosophical influence of poet Karel van de Woestijne, who developed into the first group's spiritual leader. They were introduced to the Pre-Raphaelites by Jules de Praetere, a painter, draughtsman and typographer who was a great admirer of William Morris. The mix of these different intellectual currents produced a solemn, often hieratical style that occasionally lapsed into mannerism, and which tended more towards pure, precise contours than the undefined, mellifluous nature of colour and impasto. Conversely, the artists in the second Latem group concentrated on the luminist beauty characteristic of Émile Claus, in particular Gustave de Smet, whose scenes of rustic and daily life were at times suffused with poetry. De Smet's art was later influenced by German expressionism.

It was not until after the First World War, and in different places, that the aesthetic common to the artists in the second group became established. The Sélection studio of contemporary art, then the review of the same name edited by André de Ridder and Paul-Gustave van Hecke, were central to an artistic revolution and the blossoming of Flemish expressionism between 1925 and 1930, with Constant Permeke as its figurehead.

GEORGE MINNE, Mother Weeping Over Her Dead Child, *1886*
Group, bronze, 45.5 × 16.5 × 27 cm
Inv. 6183

GEORGE MINNE, Torso of a Man, *1911–post 1913*
Torso starting at the hips, bronze, 99.5 × 89 × 38.5 cm
Inv. 4029

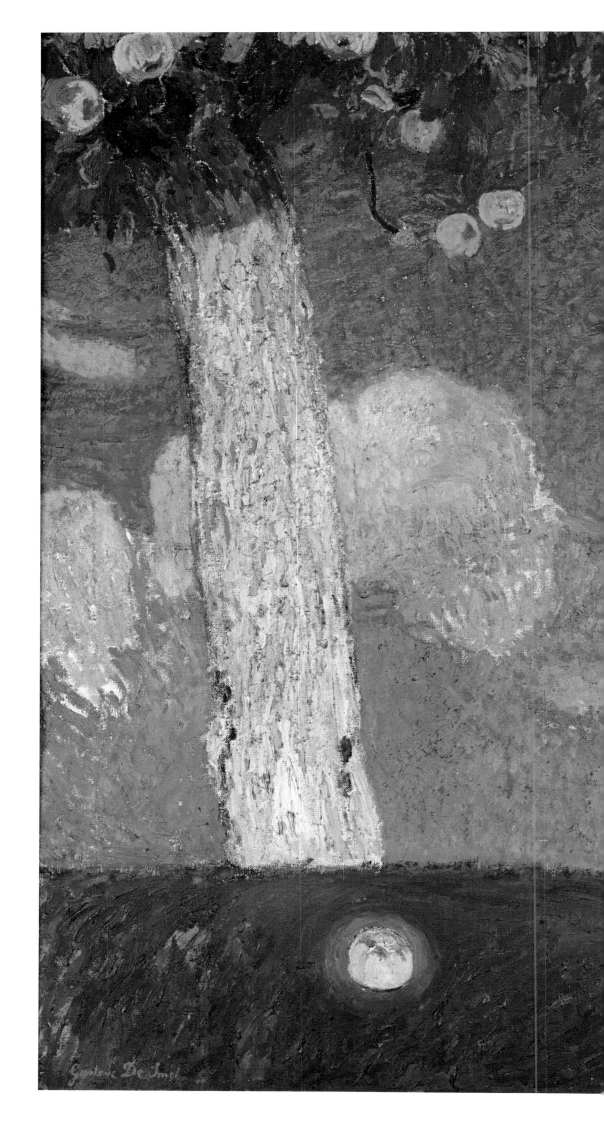

GUSTAVE DE SMET, Eve *or* The Apple, *1913*
Oil on canvas, 119 × 157 cm
Inv. 6979

Living in the artists' colony in Sint-Martens-Latem
in 1908, Gustave de Smet (1877–1943) painted
landscapes of fields, orchards and the River Lys
influenced by the luminist painting style and
centred on chromatic relationships. His works
from this period are touched by poeticism and
melancholy. De Smet later shifted to symbolist
subjects, as exemplified by this painting of
Eve in mellow colours, an attempt to suggest
the idea of desire.

PHOTOGRAPHIC CREDITS

Archives d'Architecture Moderne, Brussels: pp. 97 (top and bottom), 98 (left)

Archives de l'Art Contemporain en Belgique / Musées royaux des Beaux-Arts de Belgique: pp. 47, 60 (top and bottom), 61, 62 (top left and right), 63, 82 (bottom left and right)

Belfius Banque Collection: pp. 51, 109

Bibliotheca Wittockiana, Brussels: p. 124 (bottom)

Bibliothèque Royale de Belgique, Brussels: pp. 62 (bottom), 123

Cinémathèque Royale, Brussels: p. 99

Institut Royal du Patrimoine Artistique, Brussels: pp. 94, 96 (top), 98 (right), 105

Musée Royal de l'Afrique Centrale Collection, Tervueren / photo Alexandre, 1897: p. 116 (bottom)

Musées Royaux d'Art et d'Histoire, Brussels: pp. 32 (top and bottom), 33, 34, 35 (top and bottom)

Musées royaux des Beaux-Arts de Belgique, Brussels / photo Guy Cussac, Brussels: pp. 90 (bottom), 91, 131; Vincent Everarts Photographie, Brussels: p. 53; photo J. Geleyns / Ro scan: pp. 2, 4, 22, 23, 25, 26–27, 31, 36, 40–41, 43, 46, 48, 50, 52, 54–55, 59, 65–66, 67, 68, 70–71, 72 (top), 73, 74, 77, 78–79, 80–81, 83, 87, 90 (top), 102, 103, 104–05, 106–07, 111, 115 (top and bottom), 119 (left and right), 120–21, 124 (top), 125 (bottom), 126, 127, 128, 129, 134, 135, 137, 138, 139 (bottom), 140, 141 (top and bottom), 144, 146–47, 148, 149, 150–51, 155, 156–57; photo Grafisch Buro Lefevre, Heule: pp. 72 (bottom), 110, 116 (top), 117, 152, 154; Photo d'Art Speltdoorn & Fils, Brussels: pp. 20, 21, 28–29, 30, 37, 39, 42, 56, 58, 66, 69, 76, 82 (top), 84, 85, 88–89, 100, 101, 108, 111, 118, 130, 132, 133

Photo J. Geleyns / Ro scan: pp. 10–11, 14 (top and bottom), 16, 17, 112–13, 114, 125 (top)

Photo Bruno Piazza: p. 139 (top)

Photo Wim Robberechts & Co: p. 96 (bottom)

Photo Luc Schrobiltgen: p. 95

Université Libre de Bruxelles: p. 49

☺ SABAM Belgium 2013: pp. 46, 48, 49, 50, 51, 52, 53, 54, 77, 108, 109, 111, 1115, 124 (top), 144, 146, 148, 149, 150

The publisher has made every effort to observe the legal copyright requirements though without succeeding in identifying with certainty the origin of all the photographs reproduced. Those with a claim to make are asked to contact the publisher.

Page 2:
Théo van Rysselberghe, *The Promenade*, 1901 (detail)
Oil on canvas, 97 × 130 cm
Inv. 3745

Page 4:
Léon Spilliaert, *Bather*, 1910 (detail)
Brush and Indian ink, pastel on paper, 64.9 × 50.4 cm
Inv. 6622

© 2013, Éditions Hazan
(11, rue Paul-Bert 92247 Malakoff Cedex)
www.editions-hazan.com
© 2013, Musées royaux des Beaux-Arts de Belgique, Brussels
www.fine-arts.museum.be

ISBN 9782754107488
Dépôt légal : December 2013

Photoengraving: Reproscan, Orio Al Serio, Italy
Printing: Gruppo Editoriale Zanardi, Padua, Italy
Printed in Italy in December 2013